Praise

"A splendid look at the collective craving to beat time and space, and the competition it triggered, in the mid-nineteenth century American news business. Thoroughly researched and buzzing with lively characters, *Race to the Cape* traces the evolution of news transmission ... Theresa O'Leary has written a book of creative non-fiction that vibrates with her feelings for the harsh beauty of the Atlantic island, and its role in linking the Old and New Worlds."
CHARLOTTE GRAY, CM, *PASSIONATE MOTHERS, POWERFUL SONS: THE LIVES OF JENNIE JEROME CHURCHILL AND SARA DELANO ROOSEVELT*

"From rowboats and carrier pigeons to telegraph cables and secret codes, O'Leary's account of this transformative time is a rollicking yarn. Overflowing with unforgettable characters and tales of derring-do, her book provides vivid and important insight into a place and age that irrevocably changed the way the world communicated, and journalists worked."
GILLIAN FINDLAY, FORMER CBC AND ABC FOREIGN CORRESPONDENT, FORMER HOST CBC *THE FIFTH ESTATE*

"A fascinating, expertly told account of a forgotten but exciting chapter in the history of North American news gathering."
KARL WELLS, *OPENLY KARL*

"Theresa O'Leary's *Race to the Cape* is a tumultuous ride through the evolution of the newswire service and one man's quest for honesty, objectivity, and urgency in reporting. It's an important read in this era of post-truth politics."
STEVEN EARLE, *A BRIEF HISTORY OF EARTH'S CLIMATE: EVERYONE'S GUIDE TO THE SCIENCE OF CLIMATE CHANGE*

"O'Leary writes with historical accuracy and journalistic flair about a brief but brilliant moment in the evolution of communication technology."
KIM KIERANS, *JOURNALISM FOR THE PUBLIC GOOD: THE MICHENER AWARDS AT FIFTY*

Race
to the
Cape

THE DARING NEWS CHASE,
THE BIRTH OF THE ASSOCIATED PRESS,
& THE JOURNALIST AT THE HEART OF IT ALL

THERESA M. O'LEARY

Published by Ingenium Books Publishing Inc.
Toronto, Ontario, Canada M6P 1Z2
https://ingeniumbooks.com

International Standard Book Numbers (ISBNs):
Paperback: 978-1-990688-56-0
Ebook: 978-1-990688-57-7

Cover Design by Jessica Bell Design via Ingenium Books

For my late father, Paul Joseph O'Leary, who shared stories with me of his beloved birthplace, Portugal Cove South

and my late mother, Frances Marguerite O'Leary (née Barnes), whose love and belief in me never wavered

Race to the Cape is a work of creative nonfiction, which means everything in the book comes from fact-based research. Dialogue was created between characters to bring the story to life but the words spoken were based on the author's interpretation of the facts.

Daniel H. Craig
1881

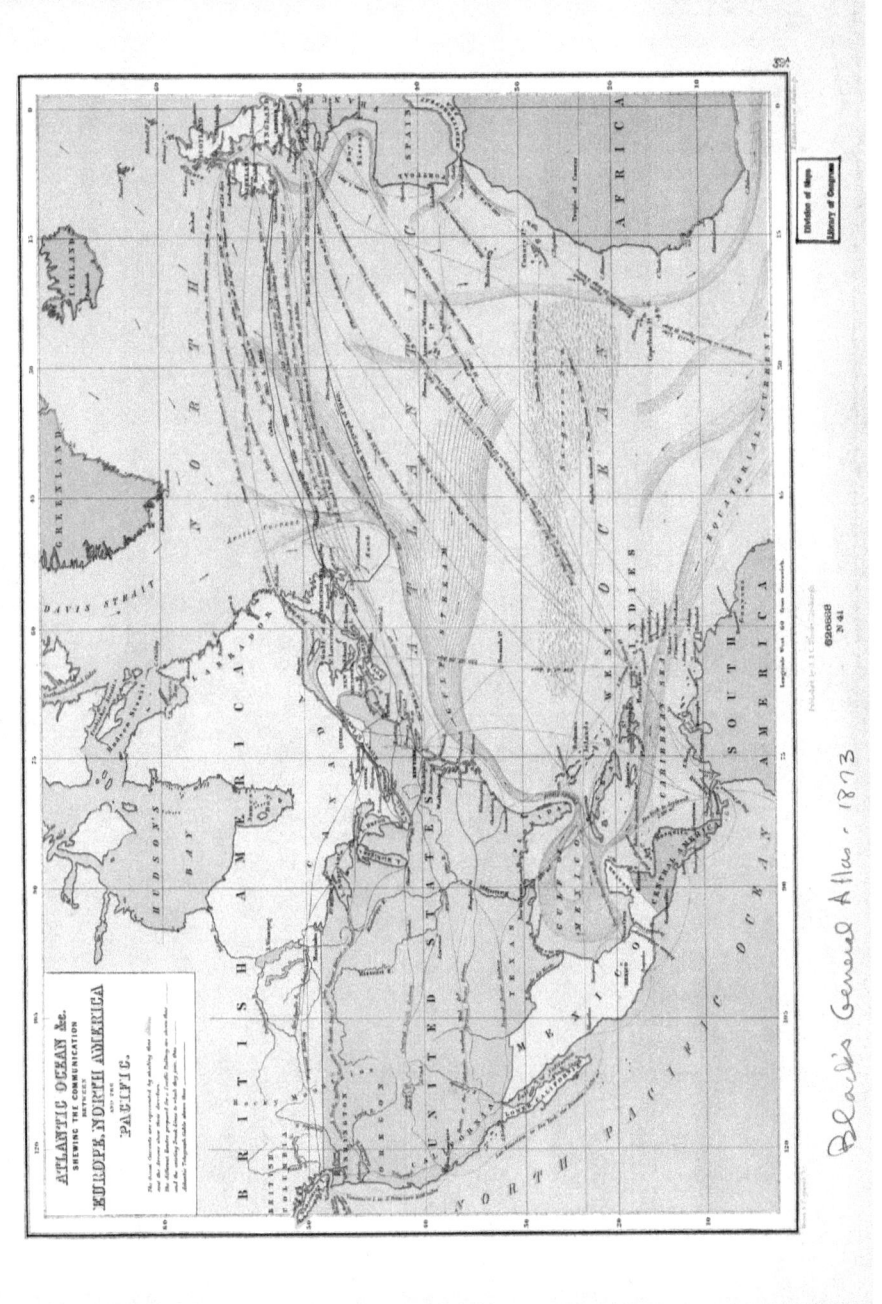

Major transatlantic communications routes
(Library of Congress, Geography and Map Division)

Table of Contents

Timeline

1837	Daniel H. Craig in Baltimore at *The Sun*
1844	Electric telegraph between Baltimore and Washington
1844	Craig moves to Boston
1846	The New York Associated Press forms loosely
1848	The NYAP forms permanently
1849	Craig hired as general agent in New York City
1851	Craig becomes general manager of the NYAP
1853	Crystal Palace Exhibition/World's Fair
1853	Atlantic Ocean's Telegraphic Plateau discovered
1854	Transatlantic cable project begins
1855	Samuel F.B. Morse visits Newfoundland
1856	Telegraph lines reach Cape Race
1856	The NYAP news boat is launched at Cape Race
1857–58	Race to the Cape begins
1858	Transatlantic telegraph succeeds and subsequently fails
1861	Scanlan and the Civil War message
1863	Wreck of the *Anglo Saxon*
1866	The transatlantic telegraph works permanently
1866	The Race to the Cape era ends

Introduction

Most of the Irish settlers in colonial Newfoundland arrived in the mid-to-late 1700s as opposed to the 1850s, when the great famine provoked a mass-migration to British North America: Canada and the United States.

That early wave of migration across the North Atlantic brought Patrick O'Leary from the Rosscarbery area of Cork in the southwest. Crop failures and English oppression pushed more and more Irish to choose the unknown of the new world. He was among hundreds of Irish men and women, young, strong, and cheap to employ by the fishing merchants.

As Patrick boarded a sailing ship destined for America, he and his fellow immigrants may have felt secure, because they were responding to advertisements for work. Others were living in the hope and belief they would find work once they landed on the shores of the new world. But the voyage across the fierce North Atlantic lasted much longer than expected, and the monotony of the unending sea was arduous. One day, months after they had left home, the vessel broke through a heavy bank of fog. Young Patrick was awestruck by the sight of land.

Everyone on board the vessel breathed a collective sigh of relief after so many days anxiously observing nothing but a distant horizon that seemed unreachable, just as a new, freer life seemed seductively out of reach. But finally, there was Cape Race in all its majesty: towering cliffs of charcoal shale, jagged edges jutting out over the vast blue ocean, the undulating plain of marshland stretching westward as far as the eye could see.

On the southern shore of the Avalon Peninsula, the southeast tip of the huge island of Newfoundland, Cape Race was first landfall in North America. It was a welcome sight to the weary travellers thirsty for a sign their desire for something better was leading them somewhere beyond hope.

The sun came out, revealing the natural beauty of Cape Race and the surrounding southern shore landscape, reminding Patrick of the ragged coast back home. He decided to end his transatlantic journey on an island sitting in the middle of the Atlantic Ocean, choosing to disembark at a lonely, remote place: a rugged, barren headland. He took in the magnificent view from the high cliffs as he walked west, for hours and hours on the boggy ground, making his way slowly in unknown rough terrain. Most days in the area it was windy, rainy, and foggy, so the walk would have been long and difficult. He was grateful for the good weather and would come to cherish every moment he wasn't soaked through.

He walked until he found Portugal Cove South, named by the Portuguese who had used it as a fishing station centuries earlier. West of the cape, tucked into a cove with not a tree in sight, there were long beaches broadening out to a distant horizon. Spotting a fisherman on the beach, Patrick strode forward and introduced himself to William Hartery, a fellow Irishman from Wexford, southern Ireland, and the founder of Portugal Cove South.

The few saltbox houses dotting the landscape looked out upon the sea, exposed to the elements. There was nowhere for the people to hide—unlike most outports along Newfoundland's coastline, where bays and coves protected residents from the intense weather and the punishing salt and humidity of the ocean.

But there was easy access to the fishing grounds, and more than enough land to dry the cod fillets once salted and laid out in the sun, either on flakes or on the long rocky beach. In those years, fishing and farming were the main work options to choose from for locals living along the south shore: Long Beach, the Drook, Portugal Cove South, Biscay Bay, and Trepassey.

Patrick settled into life in the cove. He dropped the O— which signalled he was a Roman Catholic—from his name, and was thereafter known as Patrick Leary. He married and started a family. He put his energy into working as a planter: a fisherman who headed his own inshore cod-fishing enterprise, a family affair meant to sustain them all.

Eventually his eldest child, Patrick, joined him in the work of catching food for supper each day and boatloads for the merchants buying their catch. In exchange, they received credit at the buyer's store. They did not receive cash for their fishing labour, regardless of how many fish they caught and delivered.

Patrick Leary Junior was the first of the clan to be born in the new world, and was given his father's name, as was the tradition in Irish culture. He came into the world in a two-storey wooden house, ten feet from the sea.

Living a simple life along the southern shore of Newfoundland, father and son fished together until young Patrick was old enough to marry and live on his own. Heading his own family-run fishing enterprise, he and Catherine Ryan lived next door to Patrick's parents as they raised their family and enjoyed a quiet life.

In 1844, their son Daniel was born. Patrick envisioned his son following in his footsteps and becoming a planter. When he turned twelve, Daniel would join his father at sea as an apprentice. That was the plan.

Late summer, early fall was berry-picking season and a fine time to be out on the barrens, enjoying the fine weather and the beautiful view. Gifts from Mother Nature, there were large, sweet blueberries; tiny but luscious red, sour partridge berries; and plump, juicy bakeapples, an orange-coloured berry that had nothing to do with apples.

Patrick and his clan, like others in the cove, would saunter across the spongy barrens that stretched forever out to the Atlantic, filling a bucket with berries, often a life-affirming act in a life built on surviving off the land and sea. On this massive rocky landmass, surrounded by water, the chase for the almighty codfish was the focus of life. When weather permitted, the men and boys spent their days on the ocean, jigging cod, bringing in enough for the day and more for salting and trade. The women and girls were responsible for gutting and filleting the fish, and the salting process for preservation.

Life was built around the seasons, as living off the sea demands. During the long, dark winter months when the ocean currents were ferocious and they could not get out on the water, and few ships ventured across the fierce North Atlantic, the people of the cove survived on salt fish, root vegetables, and berries.

The Learys tended their gardens, growing hardy vegetables. The supper table was generally filled with potato, carrot, turnip, cabbage, beets, and onion. They loved the greens attached to the turnip and dandelions. They owned a cow and a goat for milk and butter. The eider ducks, turrs, and ptarmigans provided a source of fresh protein, although cod was the staple, eaten every day.

It was a simple but sustainable life, and they provided for themselves whenever possible. When they could not, they traded cod for necessities such as tea, flour, sugar, molasses, rum, fishnet twine, and fabric to sew their own clothing.

It was often windy, foggy, and dismal in Portugal Cove South. In winter, some locals complained the wind was bitter enough to "cut da face off ya." But the Learys loved their beloved cove. Fog was frequent, which could drive a man to drink if the sun did not shine for days or weeks, but on summer days when the skies cleared and the sun shone, they were filled with joy and gratitude for bringing them to a place of peace and contentment.

But things changed dramatically in 1856, when the first lighthouse was erected at Cape Race. Many from the cove and Trepassey wandered the many miles to the building site every Sunday that summer to watch. Each section of iron weighed three quarters of a ton, and 800 bolts were used to screw the lighthouse together. The solidity of the structure confirmed that Cape Race was a critical point on the trade route between England and North America. It was an exciting moment in nautical safety on the high seas—a beacon of light welcoming Europeans to North America.

But some locals were more excited about the communications breakthrough that was occurring at the same time. Alongside the fifteen-metre tower, a small telegraph hut was constructed and connected to the new and revolutionary telegraph network.

It was all anyone could talk about: two significant steps forward in the human story connecting the remote and fierce North Atlantic to life in the new world.

But the Learys were among those more intrigued by the telegraph and what that would mean for Cape Race and Newfoundland, what it would mean for the people, and how they stood on the cusp of great change in such an isolated remote location, so far from the powers that be in London and New York City.

And young Daniel Leary was the ideal age to learn how to operate the telegraph, opening up a brand-new employment alternative. He could not contain his enthusiasm for being a part of it all.

"Oh, your Great Aunt Kitty knew Morse code," my father would say with pride. "She worked on the telegraph at Cape Race."

How many times did I hear that story as a child? I had no idea what it meant but it seemed important, and I admired my great aunt, Catherine or Kitty Lahey, née Leary.

A true storyteller, my dad would add with excitement, "The Associated Press had a news boat at Cape Race too ... so they could get the news from Europe faster."

The scene he described made little sense to me as a young girl.

"The ships slowed down as they passed Cape Race, and threw barrels overboard with mail and news from England." Filling my mind with images of huge wooden barrels bobbing around the ocean.

He would add, "Fishermen from the cove picked up the mail and delivered it to the telegraph station next to the lighthouse."

Years later, as a young news reporter working for the CBC Radio National News Service, Canada's public broadcaster, I became familiar with the Associated Press byline from the respected newswire service based in New York City.

Those childhood stories prompted me to conduct archival research, which confirmed some astonishing facts.

The New York Associated Press, a pioneering news service founded in the 1850s, located in the centre of the new world in New York City, had indeed stationed a boat to chase news at Cape Race, a remote headland at the southeastern tip of Newfoundland, jutting out in the Atlantic Ocean.

The story that follows reveals why Cape Race, on the edge of the North American continent, was at the centre of the Race to the Cape, a pivotal, transformative time in human communications and journalism.

Chapter 1
The Carrier Pigeon News

The carrier pigeon perched on Daniel H. Craig's left forearm rustled its feathers, its instinct for speed written in its DNA. The young man could not be as certain about the origins of his own talents in chasing news.

The morning sun shone down upon the pair, lighting up the dark-haired Craig's piercing blue eyes. He stroked the back of his avian work partner on an early spring morning in Baltimore, Maryland. He stood quietly, observing the bird observing him, its head moving back and forth, the bird scanning its surroundings.

What enabled the birds to return to their home—his home—after each flight? Was it the visual image of the house on Orleans Street that attracted the pigeons? *Homing pigeon* was the perfect moniker, the nineteenth-century newsman thought. The more Craig worked with the pigeons, the more he realized he could trust them. His respect for them grew daily, as they made him more and more effective as a news gatherer for *The Sun* in Baltimore. One of the first things his boss, Arunah S. Abell, had taught him was there is no forcing a bird to do anything, especially ones with the lineage of this flock all the way from the African continent.

Abell was only five years older than Craig, but the Baltimore news editor seemed worldly to the twenty-five-year-old from small town Rumney, New Hampshire. Abell was an experienced journeyman, a tradesman, and he owned a printing press, but his ambitions went beyond the practical trade of printing.

His friend and contemporary, Benjamin Day, had launched the first penny paper four years earlier in New York City, challenging the established belief that news was only for the wealthy business, legal, and merchant classes. The publication's novel approach to journalism focused on what was happening in New York City, including local crime and courts, fires, and weather.

Day's New York-based *The Sun* had proven successful, despite Abell's scepticism about the idea, as citizens of New York and Boston heartily embraced the penny papers. Day's success inspired Abell and two colleagues to launch a penny paper in Philadelphia.

Abell then turned his journalistic eye to Baltimore, a city of 93,000 inhabitants: a busy seaport and shipbuilding centre, established at the outbreak of the American Revolution as a port for shipping tobacco and grain. Baltimore tall ships sailed and traded as far away as the Caribbean. Abell viewed the city as turbulent and lawless, a perfect location for a newspaper reporting on local crime and other domestic matters.

The editors of the emerging penny papers were directly challenging the established way of doing things in the information distribution business. The *Journal of Commerce* was top dog and served the wealthy elite, charging six cents a paper from its location on Wall Street in Lower Manhattan.

Later renamed *The Wall Street Journal*, it focused on foreign news arriving from England and Europe via steamship, mostly news about war and politics. Whatever the news, it was presented with bias: that of the paper's masters. It was neither objective nor fact based, as it was delivered through the lens of the wealthy establishment, the upper class of the day.

One spring night in 1837, Abell and a crew of eight men, including Daniel Craig, printed 15,000 copies of a four-page tabloid. On Wednesday, May 17, the first issue of Baltimore's *The Sun* hit the streets. In it, Abell announced his intentions for the publication:

> *We shall give no place to religious controversy, nor to political discussions of merely partisan character. On political principles, and questions involving the interest and honor of the whole country, it will be free, firm, and temperate. Our object will be the common good, without regard to that of sects, factions, or parties; and for this object we shall labor without fear or partiality.*

The Sun's motto was *Light for All*, capturing Abell's mission to make his newspaper accessible to any reader, regardless of status or income.

He managed, edited, and published *The Sun* from his office at 21 Light Street, near the inner harbour of the second largest city in the United States. By the end of August, it had a circulation of 12,000 copies—twice the number of subscribers of the oldest established newspaper in the city. Two years after launching *The Sun*, the building on Light Street was no longer big enough to accommodate the staff of the growing newspaper. Abell moved his offices to the southeast corner of Gay and Baltimore streets.

Abell was happy to have Craig working alongside him, and together they organised a reliable carrier-pigeon express for the distribution of news between New York, Philadelphia, Baltimore, and Washington. *The Sun* sheltered 400–500 working news pigeons in a house on Hampstead Hill, near the old Maryland Hospital for the Insane. The messenger birds were trained to fly to incoming ships to receive the mail.

The elder man enjoyed imparting his knowledge of the news business to Craig, who was now behaving more like a journalist than a printer's apprentice, which was what he was hired to do initially. Abell often complained about the lack of local news and the fact that newspaper owners got their news from their social networks, which he didn't have, being a tradesman from Providence, Rhode Island. Sitting behind his large wooden desk in his office, he criticized the elitism driving the newspaper business. Craig sat across from him in a wooden straight-backed chair, leaning forward to take in every word.

"In New York and Boston, the men who own the papers are rich and connected. They don't have to chase news; news comes to them. If someone is launching some new industrial process or business, then they will bring that news to the newspapers. But in the penny papers," Abell said, as if he were arguing with Craig, "we chase news! We go out and find the news."

Craig's calm, cool exterior belied the fiery intellect behind his impossible-to-read face. He nodded his head in agreement. His mentor's opinions resonated deeply with him. He didn't have any patriarchal connections helping him out or bringing him important news developments occurring in the city.

Abell's training combined with Craig's natural curiosity meant Craig began reading the newspapers with a different understanding and a keen eye. He began to quickly recognize the value or importance of a piece of information, as all newspeople do.

Meanwhile, the appetite for news from the old world seemed insatiable, but the delivery of the foreign news was painfully slow. It depended upon ships steaming across the vast, dangerous Atlantic, from Liverpool, England—the major British port—to the Eastern Seaboard, in particular the coastal cities of Boston and New York City; then travelling on land via the pony express and farther via carrier pigeon. The weather was unpredictable, and stormy conditions often slowed mail delivery. From November to April, it was especially difficult for those relying on mail delivery for news from the United Kingdom, whether personal, political, or commercial. News of shipwrecks and lost ships appeared regularly in newspapers.

On a slow news day in August of 1840, Craig and Abell stood in the editor's office, both intently reading a story in the previous day's *Sun*.

Abell broke the silence. "The Brig *Florence*, travelling from Rotterdam to New York, sank off the southeast coast of Newfoundland. Fifty people lost their lives. Another deadly wreck. Cape Race is treacherous."

Craig finished reading, and looked up. "I see that cape mentioned in the papers quite a lot, but I don't know it." Craig had grown up in a town in the interior of New England, far from the Atlantic coast, and was unfamiliar with coastal topography.

Abell continued with enthusiasm. "Daniel, I've been told that Cape Race is a flat headland. Barren and bereft of life. Surrounded by massive cliffs and jutting out into the ocean. On the most easterly island on the continent."

"So, it's the first sight of land for ships from England to the eastern seaboard?"

"Yes, exactly. It is first landfall in North America."

As Craig conjured up images of the high seas and foreboding cliffs at Cape Race, he reflected, "It must be a lonely place. I wonder if Helena remembers seeing Cape Race on her way to

Boston. I'll ask her this evening. She was only five when her family crossed the Atlantic."

"It's a dreadfully long journey from what I hear," Abell said. "I hope she doesn't remember too much."

Closing his eyes momentarily, a frown transformed Craig's face.

"What is it?" Abell asked.

Lowering his voice, Craig said, "When my father died, my mother didn't know he was gone until several months later. I was a child, so I don't recall my father at all. But discovering he had been dead for months was an extra bit of sorrow for my dear mother."

"Sadly, that happens far too often." Abell cursed the challenge of communicating across distances, whether across land or ocean. "Let us hope Morse has some luck with his electric telegraph."

Samuel F.B. Morse and Abell were friends, so the *Sun* owner was aware that he was hard at work on a new communications technology that would use electricity sent along wires to transmit words.

"You know, you're not alone, Daniel. My dear friend Samuel was driven in part to work on his invention because of his own personal suffering. As a young man he went to London for a lengthy period and was separated from his parents. He felt terribly lonely and isolated."

Craig thought about the sense of isolation so many people felt in North America because it was so challenging to keep in touch with loved ones and family back in England, Ireland, Scotland, and continental Europe. Abell continued, "Samuel's first wife of twenty years, dear Lucretia, fell ill, and before he could return to her side, the poor woman was laid to rest. He had received the news too late to get home before she died."

Craig grimaced. Morse was not an engineer by training, but what he was trying to create would be an electrical engineering feat, a first in history. Many believed he would fail. Many were convinced it was impossible to use electric currents to send messages from one human to another in different locations.

"Unless Mr. Morse succeeds, the pigeon post and pony express are still the fastest ways for us to get the news on land," Craig said.

Craig had no idea, when he began working for Abell, that he would be feeding and caring for pigeons as part of his duties. But he seemed to love the challenge and threw himself into mastering communication with the birds who, despite tiny brains, were incredibly smart and lightning fast. They travelled at speeds of up to ninety miles per hour and could fly hundreds of miles without rest.

Craig felt a thrill when he set the birds free, watching them wing their way back home after completing the day's assignment. He discovered he shared the birds' instinct for speed, and together they became a force to be reckoned with in the field of news gathering.

Daniel's thirst for the foreign news matched that of Americans in general. On a personal level, many people were desperate for connection with their loved ones. On a business level, things like the price of cotton on the London stock market was a vital piece of information for investors in New York City. On a political level, there was much official communication that took place about duties and taxes.

Abell had taught Craig how to handle the avian messengers based on his own experience: how to print a short message—a news headline—on thin, tissue-like paper, taking care not to tear it. Then how to deftly roll the slim note into a tiny tube and attach it to the pigeon's scrawny leg, sending the bird flying to its next destination.

He developed a unique combination of skills: staying mentally calm and patient, and physical strength and agility to gather news. A balancing act that took nerves of steel—and Craig had just the right temperament.

Craig was a news reporter before the job existed. His ambitions coincided with a time of great change in the field of journalism. The era when people relied on newspapers as their only source of news was ending as telegraph technology was emerging.

Chapter 2
The Telegraph News

Craig and Abell left *The Sun*'s office and walked a little faster than usual toward Mount Clare Station. It was a fine spring morning in Baltimore and May 24, 1844 promised to be an historic day. The two newsmen were on their way to do their own primary research and gather the news themselves.

The air crackled with energy when they heard a din of excited voices. A mob of hundreds gathered outside the railway office. They waded through the crowd to get to the door.

"Excuse us," Abell said.

"Why do you get to go inside?" a man asked.

"We're from *The Sun*," Craig said, his hand on the door.

Alfred Vail, Samuel Morse's business partner, opened it from inside, beckoning them in. He shook their hands while exchanging pleasantries. The telegraph pioneer then turned toward the door, closing and locking it firmly in an attempt to block at least some of the noise from the public spectators.

Vail returned to the desk and started busily checking his electric telegraph instruments. And while Vail was in Baltimore, Morse was at the Supreme Court Chamber in Washington, D.C., preparing to send a short message along the newly constructed telegraph line twenty miles north to Baltimore. Construction on the telegraph link lasted a month, with the financial support of the US government.

Vail paused for a moment, his hands resting lightly on the complicated metal and wood transmitter. He turned and went back to the door. Realizing the crowd's heartfelt desire to be a part of history, he turned the lock and opened the door.

"Fifteen or so of you may come inside to watch," he called over the clamour. A wave of enthusiasm travelled through the eager group as it moved forward en masse. Craig stepped forward to help Vail close the door after the allotted number had entered. In a stern voice, Vail admonished them. "You must remain absolutely still and absolutely quiet." The thrilled observers nodded their heads in agreement.

Vail returned to the table, lowered himself onto a hard wooden office chair, and leaned over his telegraph instruments, signalling the important work was about to begin.

Twenty-two miles away in the Supreme Court Chamber in Washington, Morse took a deep breath. He tapped his telegraph key, producing a series of dots and dashes that only a few were trained to understand.

What hath God wrought?

Almost instantly, the brief quote from the Bible travelled along the thin telegraph cable held up by tall, slender wooden poles interspersed along a route between Washington and Baltimore.

Vail leaned forward, tilting his head so one ear was close enough to take in the sounds coming across the wire. As Morse's business partner, he had helped develop the language of the telegraph, so he was quite capable of translating the message by ear without having to physically write down the words.

"What … hath … God … wrought," he called out precisely and distinctly. The room erupted in excited murmurs. Watching, Craig smiled but said nothing.

Vail tapped his telegraph key, using dots and dashes to send back the same message. A confirmation of receipt as well as a test of the system. The exchange of new information had travelled across twenty-two miles, and back again, in a fraction of a second.

Morse then telegraphed a second question:

Have you any news?

Vail again called out the message as it was arriving through the telegraph, prompting gasps and whispers from the crowd.

Abell turned to Craig. "Now that's the more important question, is it not?" The speed of the telegraph clearly had the potential to satisfy the growing demand for timely news.

Craig observed the crowd and noticed that people were mesmerized by the magical electromagnetic telegraph.

Abell told Craig to stay through the morning while he returned to the office. The two newshounds shook hands. Abell caught Vail's eye as he turned into the throng of onlookers and tipped his hat in acknowledgement.

Once back at his desk, Abell put his thoughts down on paper about the significant change that had just been sparked right there in humble Baltimore.

The next morning, *The Sun* published an article on how Morse's electric telegraph annihilated time and space. Similar headlines appeared in newspapers coast to coast, and papers sold out in record time as people devoured news about the first electric telegraph line on the continent of North America. It was a technological step forward for humankind eclipsing the most recent significant advance of 1436, when German gold-smith Johannes Gutenberg invented the printing press, which naturally led to newspapers, the mainstay of journalism in the world until the electric telegraph.

The inaugural telegraph line from Washington to Baltimore had been sanctioned and funded by the US government, making the technological breakthrough official and dispelling naysayers who believed it was a hoax.

Not everyone was as certain about the electric telegraph's potential. But the proof of its power came in the realm of politics, a few days after that first telegraph.

The Democratic National Convention was taking place at Baltimore's biggest auditorium, Odd Fellows Hall. *The Sun* was paying close attention to such an important event in its city. Abell and Craig attended, making notes for the news stories that would appear the following day.

Morse had telegraphed from the Supreme Court Chamber that Washington's interest in the convention was intense; hundreds of politicians had crowded around outside the closed door to his telegraph post, awaiting word from Baltimore. As news of the raucous leadership race was delivered to Vail, he transmitted the messages south to the political centre, including the final surprising result: The dark horse candidate, James Polk, had won.

Upon arrival in Washington, members of Congress yelled out to Morse to come to the window. When he did, they cheered three times for Polk and three times for the telegraph.

A week later, Abell wrote in *The Sun*:

> *Prof. Morse's Telegraph has already, during the first week of its operations, been proved to be of the greatest public importance.*

That weekend, Craig was at home in New Jersey, sitting in his study in front of a pile of newspapers on his desk, scanning them one at a time. In *The Sun*, an editorial written by Abell caught his attention.

His boss predicted the telegraph would have a major impact on the lives of ordinary Americans. In fact, he said it was already doing so, and shared this real-life example to readers: When a train of the Baltimore and Ohio Railroad stopped at Relay, a passenger learned that his father, Mr. Godsby, had died. The news had been telegraphed ahead to the station.

The story reminded Craig of his own family's experience with learning of Craig Senior's death. It pleased him to learn that already the telegraph was helping reduce pain and suffering among Americans. By then, Craig had seven years of experience in the field of journalism, and he was certain of his own approach to news: non-partisan or fact-based, gathered and told from an objective mindset.

In the coming months, he kept track of the construction of the telegraph lines extending beyond Washington and Baltimore. From the beginning, the telegraph news operated on a twenty-four-hour cycle. News could be sent at any time of day or night, creating a sense of urgency about the arrival of any information. At least on land.

After dinner one evening at home in Baltimore, Craig broached a subject he had been thinking about all day. "When that telegraph line is laid between Manhattan and Boston, it will be worth millions. What change that will bring is hard to predict, but there will be a new world."

Helena, his wife, astute as ever, wondered aloud, "So, should we be thinking of moving back home to Boston? We could celebrate our tenth anniversary there in November." They now had a one-year-old daughter, Ida, but Helena was not tied to Baltimore. Nor was he.

Craig smiled. She always seemed to know what he was thinking before he spoke. They were a good pair, each of them the youngest of their respective family's brood of siblings, and they shared an adventurous spirit. Helena had been just five years old when her father, a stonecutter, and her mother decided to leave Portsea, Hampshire, England, and emigrate to Boston. James and Jane Croome were in their mid-forties when they gave in to the magnetic attraction of freedom and opportunity in America. It was a bold, brave step to begin again in an entirely new world.

Helena grew up on Pleasant Street in Boston, not too far from where she and Craig met, at 47 Court Street, just across from City Hall. It was where Craig worked as a printer. Helena's brother William also worked in the building, as an engraver. One day while visiting him, nineteen-year-old Helena and twenty-two-year-old Daniel crossed paths for the first time. By the end of 1834, they married, three days before Craig's birthday.

After Helena's suggestion, Craig approached Abell about moving east to Boston to be closer to the news arriving from England and Europe. *The Sun* would benefit, as it would be Craig's first priority. He planned to forge ahead as an independent news gatherer serving many clients. Abell was not in a hurry to see Craig go, as he was an asset to him right there in Baltimore, but he was certain the move would be a successful one.

Within days of the launch of the telegraph, the transformative impact on the news business was evident. Incoming telegrams were literally pasted onto broadsheets of paper and then printed and sold on Broadway in New York City. Runners—young boys, mostly—yelled their iconic sales pitch, "Extra! Extra! Read all about it!" from Battery Park, along Broadway through the Financial District in Lower Manhattan.

As long as the telegraph lines were in good working order, electrical signals could be sent from point A to point B—on land. The news media landscape had changed permanently and had intensified the news race between fierce adversaries.

The Craigs, now in their early thirties, boarded the train to travel north some 400 miles from Baltimore to Boston. They moved into a house at 16 London Street. Once settled, Daniel was hard at work using his messenger pigeons to chase news from London and Paris on the steamships arriving daily offshore of the East Coast cities. In Boston, he had a new tool in the ever-urgent chase for news: a rowboat. His work life revolved around the boat, the birds, and the telegraph office.

Chapter 3
The Rowboat News

Boston Harbor in the early morning, a hired rowboat, and a basket of pigeons—Craig's new habitat. He felt the boat lurch underneath him as he carefully laid the small basket at his feet. His secret weapons in his relentless pursuit of new information.

Helena was his work partner in the rowboat news, in addition to caring for their young daughter. She had become accustomed to living with a cage full of pigeons, and learned to communicate with them as she fed them and cleaned their living quarters. Craig had trained her how to hold out her gloved forearm, providing them with a place to land when they returned home with messages.

But the daily early-morning rowboat trips were Daniel's domain alone. Some days there was a light fog blanketing Boston, but frequently there was a fierce northeasterly wind that whipped through the harbour. On those days, the rowboat ride made for a punishing trip. But this morning he appreciated the softness of the foggy air on his face as the boat left the fast-growing city behind and moved slowly toward the narrow entryway to the eastern seaboard of the Atlantic.

He sat up straight, his eagle eyes piercing through the mist, and observed the man rowing the boat, getting him closer to his first capture of the day. He loved being the first to get to the massive steamships for Cunard Lines arriving daily with mail from England.

Europe and North America existed in two different worlds, isolated from one another, linked only by the ships steaming back and forth across the Atlantic. Mail for governments, commerce, and individuals could take seven to ten days if the seas cooperated. But the delivery of timely mail could not always be relied upon. Sometimes it took weeks or even months to make it across the ocean. Sometimes the mail never arrived at all due to a shipwreck.

For four years, Craig's daily routine was the same. He would get up before the sun rose, and feed himself and the pigeons. Just before he opened the door to leave home, he would open the cage, select half a dozen birds, and gently place them in a basket slung over his shoulder. Then he had to make his way to Long Wharf, where he would step into the rowboat.

It was a short ride to the deep Atlantic waters just outside Boston Harbor. Most mornings, he found several long liners from Liverpool, England, floating there, waiting for the harbourmaster to send a pilot boat to accompany them safely from the Atlantic Ocean to the inner harbour, where they could anchor or moor at the wharf.

The ships carried official mail packets from the Imperial government in England, news from warfronts in Europe, and the London stock market price of goods.

The invention of the steam engine had sparked a new shipping era. It was another industry driven by speed. Shipping magnates felt as compelled to push for faster service as the newspaper owners from Baltimore to New York City to Boston.

Craig's instincts drove him forward, gathering the news and selling it to whomever would buy the information: Wall Street speculators, telegraph owners, and newspaper editors.

Craig literally followed in the footsteps of Bostonian Samuel Topliff Jr., credited with being the man who first started systematic gathering of the news in 1811.

Frustration at not knowing what was going on in the old world had led Bostonians to create a new system for sharing the latest news about weather, trade, and what was happening in England and Europe.

Samuel Gilbert co-owned the Exchange Coffee House at the wharf in Boston. The seven-story building was the tallest in the city. It was a place where merchants and shipmasters met to exchange information as they relaxed in the Reading Room on the second floor.

To encourage their patronage, Gilbert provided two over-sized leather books filled with the latest marine intelligence and any other news of import to patrons, merchants, and shipmasters. They were called the *Marine and General News Books*, and anyone was welcome to drop in to read them, including local citizens.

The coffeehouse became the place to go to find out the most recent information arriving from across the Atlantic, and its idea of recording news was so popular that loyal customers donated a rowboat to the Reading Room.

Gilbert was then forced to hire Topliff to keep up with the demand. The young man was chasing the news regardless of weather every day, rowing out to the sailing ships and coming back directly to write it up.

The patrons of the Reading Room, knowing the risks that Topliff took to bring back the news, toasted him for his courage in doing so in an often inhospitable climate.

The rowboat news chase currently driving Craig had begun several decades earlier, when he was a child and had no idea what the future held for him. His life and work were now centred around a daily run for new information to satisfy the seemingly endless demand for news among Bostonians and New Yorkers alike.

He had scored a great contract with Wall Street investor Jacob Little, who was anxious to receive the latest information on the price of cotton on the London Stock Exchange. The steamships arrived in Boston first, giving Craig an advantage.

But he understood New York was the centre of trade and news. It is where the six most powerful newspaper barons lived, controlling the *New York Herald*, the *New-York Tribune*, the New York-based *The Sun*, the *Journal of Commerce*, the *Courier and Enquirer*, and the *New York Evening Express*. They also had rowboats stationed at the wharf in Boston, travelling to the ships outside both harbours. But to ensure they were first with the news, they would buy information from Craig. Freelancing meant he could serve many masters—and he was eager to do so.

Craig had been reading the papers daily for some time now, and it was clear to him that the newspaper owners and editors running journalism in New York City and Lower Manhattan did not entertain the idea of reporting in an objective or unbiased manner. They were opinion-driven and served different segments of the news market.

The *Journal of Commerce* was run by David Hale and Gerard Hallock. Its readers were affluent investors in the Wall Street Stock Exchange.

They did things differently, breaking tradition by placing the biggest news of the day on the front page of the newspaper. To assure subscribers that they were getting the foreign news as fast as possible, the paper started running headlines emphasizing the details of the speed with which they were delivering the news:

25 DAYS LATER FROM EUROPE.

The letters were capitalized to attract the reader's eye.

The *New York Herald* was owned and edited by James Gordon Bennett, Sr. Bennett not only conducted the first-ever newspaper interview while covering a sensational murder case in 1836—a case which also led him to pioneer the extra edition—but in 1839 was granted an exclusive interview with President Martin Van Buren: the first of its kind with a sitting president of the United States.

The Sun was started in 1833 by Benjamin Day, but by the 1840s was owned and run by Day's brother-in-law Moses Yale Beach, a shrewd businessman who was one of the wealthiest and most influential people in the city. He kept a flock of carrier pigeons in a special house on top of the newspaper's building—a common practice among publishers and editors of the day. Beach's ideas about journalism and news reporting, like those of his peers, were evolving from opinion-based news to objective journalism. Craig could see the shift as it was occurring.

From his base in Boston, Craig found himself drawn to New York, to be a part of it, until he heard stories about the violence occurring between the competing news gatherers on the water. Apparently, the rowboat men in New York were returning to their offices bleeding from their heads, mouths, and noses, with no news to show for it.

Playing dirty in the news game, they had resorted to firing belaying pins—metal or wooden pins with a rounded top, used for securing rigging lines on sailing ships—at one another on the water. Using a slingshot, the men flicked the small pins as they approached one another in their rowboats, en route to gather news from the steamships offshore. The pins were only six to twelve inches long but fired with enough force, they could cause serious injury to the eyes or face.

Craig was dismayed that the pursuit of the foreign news had descended into cutthroat competition. He might have been called pugnacious by his critics, but he was not a violent man and had never had to resort to such behaviour.

The race for news in New York had become so aggressive that some of the men running the city's papers set up a meeting. Many were from well-mannered New England and found the violence distasteful. They resolved to clean up the business by creating a harbour combine—a cooperative method for them all to get important news in a timely manner.

By pooling resources and paying for one news summary for all involved, there would be no need for such aggression. The pursuit of journalism in the new world was laying a foundation for the formation of the Associated Press as rivals came together because of shared values and the non-violent collection of news.

But that did not mean the newspapers stopped competing with one another, intensely chasing the news to get it first.

The hard-driving Craig was no less competitive—and was about to impress everyone in the field, using a trinity of tools: carrier pigeons, the humble rowboat, and the telegraph.

Chapter 4
The Unbeatable Daniel Craig

On November 16, 1846, a petite woman wearing a black dress boldly opened the door to the offices of the Magnetic Telegraph Company near the wharf, surprising the four men inside. Women rarely appeared at their office. Francis O. J. Smith was known to be a ladies' man, so he didn't mind or object. Nor did the others. She held the hand of a young black-eyed girl, and in her other hand she carried a message intended for transmission via the telegraph.

The mysterious woman insisted on being admitted to the inner office where, atop wooden tables, sat the powerful telegraph keys. This new communication tool was compact: a simple wooden bar with a knob on top and an electrical contact on the bottom. Operators pumped the key rapidly, sending out a string of dots and dashes.

The woman proffered the small note she clutched in her hand to the operator. It was addressed to Jacob Little, known as the great Wall Street operator and the magnate of Wall Street.

The subject of the message was likely the highly sought-after price of cotton on the London markets. But it was written in code—and not Morse code. The unrecognizable scribble was signed *H.C. Daniels*. This Daniels had developed his own code to prevent anyone else from interpreting the news flying along the lightning-fast lines between Boston and the Financial District of Manhattan. The woman did not move from the operator's side until she received confirmation the news had been received in New York City.

After she and the girl left the office, Smith received word that the steamship, the *Acadia*, had been sighted off Boston, arriving from Liverpool with the foreign news, which almost always included the value of cotton stocks from the London market. His staff began preparing to receive and fire off an onslaught of messages from the newly arrived steamer. They waited until an interminable thirty minutes passed and, finally, a representative entered the office, carrying a digest of the European news. As the operators started typing the information, using Morse code and their telegraph keys, the keys failed. They pumped the electro-magnetic devices up and down, but nothing was happening. It was clear something was wrong. Smith sent staff to inspect the line, and they reported the telegraph wire had been cut about four miles west of Boston.

Communication to New York was not possible. Barely able to contain his anger, Smith barked at the operators that the line would not be up and running again until the next morning.

Smith had been fighting Morse and others in court over telegraph rights since the advent of the technology. He was a cantankerous and litigious man who even Morse called vile and hateful. Smith had an inkling that the woman who had delivered the message from H.C. Daniels was Helena Craig. He thought Daniel Craig was a man of questionable character who would cut a telegraph line to prevent others from using it.

He walked to the Boston courthouse and filed a lawsuit against the rowboat newsman.

"As if I needed to cut wires to be the first with the foreign news." Daniel had broken the silence between them as he and Helena were out walking along the wharf. It was a pleasant evening: cool temperatures and just a slight breeze.

Helena nodded her head. "Exactly, my dear. Everyone knows you are an honest, hard-working man with integrity."

Craig did his best to ignore the drama, although the lawsuit meant he had to deal with it in court. He knew he was innocent, and others in the field concurred, so he was confident nothing would come of Smith's accusations. And he was right. Smith was unable to provide evidence that Craig was responsible for severing the line.

Then, in early 1847, four months after the first intriguing visit, the petite woman in the black dress appeared at the Magnetic Telegraph Company office again, with another message. This one was also addressed to Jacob Little. And within a short time of her visit, once again, the lines to New York were cut.

Some speculated it was Little himself who had cut the lines, or that he had hired someone to do it. After all, Smith reasoned, the investor had a reputation as an unscrupulous cutthroat. But no one was ever able to determine, definitively, who was behind the sabotage of the lines.

Chapter 5
The Fact-Based News

It was a short walk from the *Journal of Commerce* office to the *New York Herald* in the Financial District of Lower Manhattan. David Hale, owner of the *Journal*, knocked on the door, a tall hat upon his head. As he waited for someone to appear, he looked around, marvelling at the construction occurring. The city was growing fast and growth in the new world was noisy.

Men in formal suits and ties walked quickly past him, tipping their hats to one another as they conducted their business with determination and confidence.

From inside, the *Herald*'s owner's voice called out, "Come in!" Hale entered, and James Bennett stood up behind his heavy wooden desk, cluttered with papers, to welcome his normally aloof competitor.

Hale met Bennett's eyes, although it was challenging to make direct eye contact with the cross-eyed man. With raised brows, Bennett waited for his visitor to speak and explain this sudden appearance in his office. It was not every day the two men engaged in conversation about anything, given they were from different worlds and served opposite markets: One informed the wealthy, and one informed the working population. But today Hale had gone out of his way to visit his competitor. Bennett's natural curiosity was piqued.

Like most newsmen, the editor of the *Journal* got right to the point. "I have called to talk about the current state of our news business with you. Do you have any objection?"

Bennett adjusted his spectacles and nodded toward a hard-backed chair. When Hale was comfortably seated, his host filled the silence.

"What are you concerned about? Losing the news race?" The former Scotsman may have thought he was being funny, but he seemed to be living up to his reputation for being almost obnoxiously inquisitive. Bennett knew that Hale did not like him. That didn't bother him. Respect was better than popularity, and he knew the *Herald*'s success meant he had that from his peers. They both knew he was considered the most daring of the news gatherers, with a seemingly magic touch.

No one could deny that Bennett was the fastest and most ingenious in getting the news. He used any and all methods of transport and communication available to him, including railroads, barges, and runners.

Bennett had created his own method for receiving reports from the war that had just begun between the United States and Mexico over the American annexation of Texas: a pony express that ran from New York City all the way to the border with Mexico. Bennett had managed it with the cooperation of Abell, Daniel Craig's old boss at *The Sun* in Baltimore, and editors at the *Public Ledger* in Philadelphia—another newspaper Abell had co-founded—and *The Picayune* in New Orleans.

Bennett did not mind letting people know when he had won his latest contest. He was cocky and boastful about his triumphs.

"Is Moses worried the *Herald* will beat *The Sun*? Is that what brought you here today?" Both men knew that Beach was conducting his own secretive chase for the news from the front with *The Sun* of New York. News dispatches were sent from Veracruz, Mexico, by boat to Mobile, Alabama. From there, an express rider employed by Beach took the dispatches to Montgomery, Alabama, beating the US mail coach. In Montgomery, the dispatches were mailed to Richmond, Virginia, and taken to the telegraph terminus.

Beach was so driven to win the news chase during the war he refused to compensate his riders for their efforts unless they delivered the news to him twenty-four hours ahead of the mail arriving for everyone else.

Hale's furrowed brow signaled to Bennett his instincts had been correct.

"I am concerned about this relentless campaign to be the first with news from the front. I am quite tired of the dangerous methods and intense competition between all of the New York papers."

Bennett listened intently to his competitor's concerns but said nothing. Hale said he had been observing Bennett's expensive activities, and the others felt things were getting out of control.

The electric telegraph made it possible to send the latest war news quickly north from Virginia to New York City. But it was a new technology, and fees were costly.

"Don't you agree that coverage of the war is so vital that we, perhaps, should cooperate rather than compete while informing the public of such important events?"

Bennett nodded. "You have no argument with me about the high cost of using the new technology. But how do you propose we do it then? Newspapers are built to compete."

Hale smiled in agreement. "That is certainly true. But the harbour combine helped reduce the violence occurring in the rowboat news. So perhaps at times cooperation works." He admitted that he had already consulted with Beach at *The Sun*, who had agreed with him, saying it was obvious that it was time to rethink the game.

"So what exactly are you proposing, Mr. Hale?" Bennett asked as he squinted.

Hale breathed deeply and leaned forward, "The only solution in the case of the Mexican conflict, in my opinion, is to pool our resources and pay the telegraph fees for just one report from the front for the top newspapers in New York."

How satisfying it must have been for Bennett being approached directly by Hale, the voice of Wall Street and capitalists, to work with the other New York City publishers for the good of them all, financially.

A newcomer to America, Bennett never really fit in with the New Englanders controlling the newspapers. But he was first and foremost a shrewd businessman and was quick to respond. "I do agree with Mr. Beach and yourself about the fact the telegraph seems to be changing everything. It's difficult to see the future. But there's no doubt we have to adapt to changing times."

He thought of the growth of his own newspaper, which had become indispensable in a shifting society.

Hale nodded. "Yes, we must adapt to new technology or die."

At the time, there was a general conviction among news editors and book publishers that literacy was essential to republican citizenship. And the growing population they were serving in all of the papers was in fact becoming more literate due to the increasing number of schools and colleges in the city and country.

Hale seemed satisfied as he rose from his seat and held out his hand. "I will be in touch soon about a meeting at *The Sun*'s offices to discuss the matter further, but it pleases me to know we agree on the basic principle of cooperation."

Bennett stood, offering his hand and an energetic handshake. It was a unique proposal: Not every day do fierce competitors decide to work together for the common good.

Bennett came around the desk and walked Hale to the door. "Thank you for including me in the plan for the Mexican–American War. But to be clear, it does not mean I won't be as hard a competitor on other news."

Hale smiled a wry smile as he left the building and returned to his office. He understood Bennett's comment, being a hard-driving newsman himself. It was a successful meeting, and it began a two-year period of a cooperative and loose association of the six main presses in New York City: the *New York Herald*, the *Journal of Commerce*, *The Sun*, the *New-York Tribune*, the *Morning Courier and New-York Enquirer*, and the *New York Evening Express*.

As promised, the editors of the newspapers met at *The Sun's* offices—a nod to the leadership of Beach in the quickly changing journalism environment. They all sat around the table, arguing and debating and finally hashing out how the system for getting news from the Mexican warfront would work: They would all pay into a general fund for the receipt of only one telegraph message with the latest military news. It meant they would all receive the same news dispatches about the war at the same time.

There would be no opinions expressed in the reports arriving via telegraph, only factual information about the conflict's progression. This collaboration of competitors would organically create the non-partisan, neutral, or objective voice in journalism, although it's doubtful they fully appreciated that at the time. The frugal mindset was driving the decisions being made.

They also agreed to collaborating on the fees to receive political news from Washington. But at this stage, no one was thinking about a long-term arrangement to cover all important events. The land-based telegraph was rapidly expanding but it still only ran to a few cities, limiting transmission opportunities.

In the beginning, this agreement amongst the six newspapers was meant to be a temporary fix to overcome the immediate problem of high telegraph fees while bringing news of the Mexican–American conflict to their readers. There was no thought of benefitting anyone but the six newspapers. They were not doing it to provide a great public service.

The system worked well in terms of getting the latest war news at a reasonable cost. In its first year, Hale started envisioning a possible union of New York's foremost newspapers. For months he met quietly with individual editors to discuss the idea, knowing that it would be difficult to persuade them to put aside their differences for the common good.

Then one lovely spring afternoon in 1848, Hale corralled the independent-minded men running New York City's most influential newspapers together to discuss managing news-gathering in the future.

Moses Beach, a key player in the transformation taking place in journalism, once again hosted the meeting at *The Sun*'s offices. Seated around the plain rectangular table sat David Hale and Gerald Hallock representing the *Journal*, the *Herald*'s James Gordon Bennett Sr. and his assistant Frederic Hudson, the *Tribune*'s Horace Greeley, James Watson Webb and Henry Raymond of the *Courier and Enquirer*, and Erastus and James Brooks from the *Express*.

Each of these men ruled their own little fiefdom in the city's newspaper industry and anything other than fierce competition would have been unthinkable. But on this day, after much argument and consternation, they surprised themselves. Their common interests won out over their competitive natures.

Hale led the meeting, arguing for making a concerted effort to offer readers more comprehensive coverage of world events.

Telegraph fees were being driven higher and higher by telegraph companies involved in their own bitter legal conflicts. Hale worried the price was going to keep rising. "With no government supervision," he told the group of news editors, "newspapers will be forced to surrender the vital function of news gathering, and the news itself will become merely a commodity, unreliable and purely commercial."

Another major concern was the fact that there was still only one telegraph line available to all the New York newspapers. The terminus of the line was in New Jersey, across the Hudson River. Each newspaper could use the line for fifteen minutes at a time to send their news. And each paid the full rate. It just made no business sense.

So, the six agreed: If they had an organization that gathered the telegraph news for all of them at the same time, it would benefit each of their newspapers.

It was at this pivotal meeting that the owners and editors gave the new group a formal name: the New York Associated Press (NYAP), an innovation in news arriving from the telegraph, a newswire agency serving many different clients or newspapers.

They incorporated the NYAP and would cover all important news, including the foreign news arriving by steamship from England. There was no telegraph connecting the continents yet, so mail delivery was still arriving by ship. To the east of the city, just outside Sandy Hook, steamships waited patiently for the pilot boat to escort them into New York Harbor.

The NYAP board of directors decided they could only afford to hire one man to carry out the work: Alexander Jones, a medical doctor by training but with some experience in news gathering on both sides of the Atlantic. As the pioneering general agent, he was expected to find and set up an office and to collect and distribute the news.

Jones quickly selected an office on the fourth floor of a building on Liberty Street. He noted that regrettably each day, his new job would start with a climb up four flights of stairs in a dimly-lit stairwell. However, the room where he worked was large. More importantly, the price was right; rent was under $500 a month. Jones's salary was $20 a week.

The NYAP's infant news operation cost between $10,000 and $20,000 in its first year. That included an assistant to share the workload. Payment for foreign news was the largest single expense, as most news that mattered still happened in England and Europe.

And accessing that news was crucial.

From his base in Boston, Daniel Craig was observing the shift toward a wire-driven news system in New York. He was doing a fine business chasing the foreign news arriving on long liners because he was located closer to Europe than New York was. Craig was well known to Bennett, Beach, and the other editors. He had beaten them many times in delivering vital news from the steamships. Bennett often referred to him as unbeatable.

One of the first things the NYAP did was to charter a boat called the *Buena Vista* to intercept all vessels arriving from Europe at Halifax, Nova Scotia. The boat's job was then to obtain the latest news and rush it south to Boston, where it could be telegraphed to the NYAP.

There was not yet a telegraph line connecting New York City and Halifax. Unbeknownst to Bennett and the NYAP, Craig secretly started using the *Buena Vista* to travel north along the eastern seaboard to Halifax, where he would intercept the delivery meant for the NYAP.

With a spring in his step, he would walk the wharf in downtown Halifax and hire a rowboat to take him to the steamships anchored in the harbour. He would speak to captains and crew for any urgent news and then read any newspapers or the European news digest on board.

Craig did not want to be recognized by anyone who might know the NYAP directors, so he would keep to himself. Once on board for the return trip south, he would stay in his cabin, working, reading all the news he had collected, and writing short messages on small slips of tissue paper to insert them into the tiny tubes attached to his pigeons' legs.

Craig would be ready to send the messengers up in the sky as soon as the Massachusetts coastline emerged on the horizon, their wings flapping frantically as they flew home to their destination.

Helena, pregnant with their second child, knew when the *Buena Vista* was scheduled to arrive and would go to the wharf, awaiting the birds' arrival regardless of the weather. She demonstrated that she was a worthy partner and able competitor. Perhaps she had her own news instincts—that inner compulsion to chase information. Perhaps she simply enjoyed the intrigue.

Helena's motivations for helping with the carrier-pigeon and rowboat news were not as clear as her husband's, but she understood the importance and urgency of getting the news to the telegraph office for transmission to clients in New York.

Many days, at an early hour, she would be at the wharf to receive a pigeon on her gloved forearm. She would gently retrieve the tube from the bird's claws. She would then immediately take off at a quick pace for the telegraph office to transmit the most recent news and information from Europe.

In New York, Bennett was more frustrated than ever with Craig's ability to beat him. He sent a telegram off to the *Buena Vista*'s captain, ordering him to capture Craig's birds the next time he boarded at Halifax, to prevent him from sending out a pigeon post.

But the wily Craig was well ahead of his competitors in New York.

"I went on deck and flew the bird close to the captain's head," he would later recall. The captain's eyes narrowed as the pigeon flew past. He ran into his stateroom and grabbed his rifle, but before he had a chance to fire a shot at the pigeon, the bird was a mile above him, well on its way to deliver Craig's message.

As Craig recounted this story to Helena at home over dinner later that evening, he laughed with glee. "I had a feeling Bennett would be up to something, so I tucked one valuable bird in my pocket as I boarded."

When Bennett and the NYAP board learned of Craig's escapades, they were displeased at first. But Bennett had to admit that the younger man in Boston had something he valued: grit, determination and something undefinable that enabled him to be the first with the news. He had to admire the man.

The outcome was that the NYAP hired Craig directly to work as a news agent in Halifax, establishing the group's first office on foreign soil, in British North America.

After working freelance for several years in Boston, Craig knew the centre of the newspaper industry was New York City.

It had likely crossed his mind that someday he would end up working there. He observed with interest the shift to a newswire agency and recognized it would change journalism along with changing technologies. He wanted to be a part of it and was happy to move closer to the arriving steamships, a key to his continued success.

Chapter 6
The New York Associated Press's Halifax Pony Express

It was early 1849, and Craig was hard at work for the NYAP, chasing the news from the steamers docking at Halifax. Most days, he could be seen standing outside the telegraph office on Hollis Street. His eyes were laser-focused on the wide harbour where he could easily spot the mail ships arriving. Getting the European news before anyone else was so important that he would spare no amount of money or effort in its pursuit.

But the telegraph lines from New York ended at Saint John, New Brunswick. They had not yet reached Halifax. So, to ensure speedy transmission, the NYAP and Craig created a pony express covering about 150 miles southwest to Digby, Nova Scotia.

Steamers were arriving in Halifax every two weeks generally, and the dispatch riders never knew when they would get there so were always on alert, like Craig, to the arrival of a new vessel carrying mail. They had to be ready to start no matter the hour, and the same alertness was requisite in furnishing fresh horses at the relay posts.

On February 21st, 1849—in the depths of winter—the first pony express was ready to leave Halifax after the arrival of

Cunard's RMS *Europa*, which had departed Liverpool, England, eleven days earlier.

Craig gave a handwritten dispatch with the latest news from the London stock market to a rider. As always, it was done in code. In a letter to the *New Brunswick Courier*, L.R. Darrow, who was manager of the New Brunswick Electric Telegraph Company, would give an example:

Boards advanced one fourth penny, Shingles 2 to 3
shillings per quarter, Lower qualities Fish 6 pence lower.

In other words, the price of cotton was up by a quarter of a cent; Indian corn was valued at two to three shillings per bundle; and flour was down by six pence.

The horseman immediately departed and rode northwest to Kentville, travelling just over sixty miles in about eight hours. Every twelve miles, he changed horses.

At the tiny fishing community of Digby, he handed over the dispatches to the mail officer on board a chartered steamboat, which was waiting to bring the latest news across the fifty miles of the Bay of Fundy to Saint John.

Once across the bay, the operators in New Brunswick telegraphed the news to Calais, Maine, and it travelled farther south along the telegraph lines to Boston and New York, several days ahead of the arrival of the European mail steamers in the United States.

Excitement ramped up in early June when Craig landed a juicy piece for the NYAP: the news of an assassination attempt on Queen Victoria in London.

Fifth assassination attempt on Queen Victoria, London,
May 19. Irishman William Hamilton fired pistol at her

majesty while she was riding in an open carriage with three of her children in Hyde Park. No one was hurt.

Charged with treason, Hamilton was angry about the Great Hunger, which had forced him out of his homeland. He used gunpowder instead of a bullet, explaining to police that he wanted to go to prison where he would get food.

When Craig learned this shocking news from a captain on board a recently arrived steamship from Liverpool, it lit a fire under him. He quickly wrote down key details about the attempted violence against the Queen, and located one of the NYAP's horsemen standing by for dispatches.

As the horseman mounted the steep hill and took off on the crucial assignment, Craig leaned back against the telegraph office wall and grinned like a Cheshire Cat.

The whole service from Halifax to Saint John and by wire to New York was called the Halifax Express. It only lasted a short nine months because it consistently revealed the need for the telegraph lines to be extended farther north to Halifax, the Queen's chosen mail delivery point on the east coast and therefore a location where much news from the old world could be gathered.

By November, the telegraph network had been extended to Sackville, New Brunswick, and then on to Halifax. That advance brought an end to the NYAP's pony express in Nova Scotia, but the inventive strategy foretold the extremes to which Craig and the NYAP would go.

One day Craig was standing outside the Hollis Street telegraph office when an operator stepped outside and handed him a telegram from New York. He glanced at the message from his bosses. They wrote that he was needed urgently at the NYAP headquarters on Broadway.

The next morning, Helena—along with six-year-old Ida and infant William—saw him off at the train station, both of them excited about what offer might await him in New York.

On the train rattling southward, Craig pondered the possibilities for the telegram.

Helena had speculated that he would be offered a position in New York. "Daniel, don't you think it has always been inevitable that we would end up in New York? The city is exploding thanks to the telegraph."

Throughout the past fifteen years of journalism, he had followed his instincts in leaving Baltimore to work in Boston and then to work in Halifax. Perhaps she was right, and he would end up in New York City, the centre of it all, where the directors of the NYAP were leading the way. Or so he thought.

Chapter 7
Building the New York Associated Press

It was early in the morning in the metropolis of Manhattan as Craig paused on his walk to work. His eye caught sight of the silhouette of Trinity Church's stoic steeple, the historic religious centre of the rapidly expanding city. The full moon was still up, lighting his path as he turned toward the New York Associated Press office at 83 Liberty.

Most of the 600,000 or so citizens calling New York City home were in bed, asleep. The only sounds at that wee hour of the morning were the plaintive cries of seagulls and crows, a din familiar to mariners and wharf rats who spend their days on waterfronts.

The headquarters of the NYAP, still in its infancy, was where the thirty-eight-year-old man would transition from extraordinary news gatherer to pioneer in objective journalism, managing the gathering and distribution of new information across the continent. Craig had loved being out in the field chasing news, but after more than a decade racing around as a freelancer with a basket of carrier pigeons in rowboats, he was now anchored to an office as a general agent for the NYAP. He had one client—his employer—and a monthly salary.

He turned his gaze eastward, where he heard some activity. The East River bustled with the noisy action of trade and construction from dawn to dusk; hammers hammered nails and saws sawed wood, shrill tweets from ship whistles and loud male voices cut through the quiet as steamships arrived one after another in the inner harbour. The rich cacophony of sounds on the docks were familiar to Craig. After a nostalgic moment of reflection, the new general agent for the NYAP resisted the urge to run to discover which vessels were arriving and what news they carried.

Instead, with some effort he pushed open the large wooden door of his office building in Lower Manhattan and looked up the long flight of stairs before starting to climb them. There were exactly seventy-eight steps between him and the office at the top. He knew that to be true because he had walked up this dimly lit stairway every day, sometimes twice a day, since he began working for the NYAP the year before, in 1850.

His colleague, Alexander Jones, had chosen an excellent location for a news service, sitting as it did between the Hudson and the East Rivers, and just a few blocks from the Battery at the southern tip of the island of Manhattan. But the office was on the fourth floor and there were days when Craig cursed that choice. He was as energetic as ever, but he was not as spry as he had been when chasing news in rowboats. The start of each day began with a heart-pumping climb to work.

There were other things that bothered Craig right from the beginning. As Craig began working with Jones and an assistant, he was not impressed, and he did not hesitate to tell his bosses that the operation felt like an amateur one: underfunded with no vision.

Jones had complained that the weekly allowance of fifty dollars for administrative expenses was not enough and that he was kept busy day and night, including on Sundays and holidays. Craig and Jones seldom retired before 1:00 a.m., and they were still expected to be at work early each morning.

The problem in Craig's mind stemmed from the original intention of the NYAP: The owners wanted to save money for their own publications, so they were starting from a limited mindset.

As he opened the door to the dingy office, it was dark and cold, so he immediately struck a match to light the kerosene lamp. Jones had not arrived yet. Craig thought to himself that the hard-working man must have needed an extra hour in bed, and he certainly deserved it.

Craig surveyed the large office, sparsely furnished with wooden tables supporting several electric telegraph keys which were now coming to life and making their distinctive sounds. Keeping his coat on for warmth, he sat down in his chair and pulled himself flush to the table, moving his telegraph key into place for the day's work.

News was already arriving from Boston and other easterly points, and he began with a message from the Halifax Telegraph Office dated February 23.

The steamship America *has arrived from Liverpool. She sailed thence on Saturday the 9th. The news is of the highest interest to the merchants and politicians. There has been no change in cotton.*

The price of cotton on the London Stock market was a key piece of news Craig was looking for every day. This news was from two weeks before, so it could have changed since then, but it was the most up-to-date information on the subject and was therefore set as currently correct.

From the Boston Telegraph Office, there was news of trouble in France:

> *Series of riots in Paris. The city in a state of siege. The destruction of trees planted during the revolution.*

Within half an hour, a yawning Jones opened the door and walked into the office. "Good morning, Craig," he said.

Craig was engrossed in his work but briefly said, "Morning, Jones." Some days were like that in the daily news business: Just keep your head down and diligently focus on the job at hand. Documenting daily life was a detailed matter in order to record history accurately. And Craig was a stickler for the facts.

Jones removed his gloves and hat, laying them at the other end of the table where he sat down and set to his tasks. It was one of those days, he could tell already, of nuts and bolts, basic information, simple yet critical information for merchants and citizens.

> *Shipping Intelligence: Antwerp, Feb 1-Arr Koophandle, NYork, Bordeaux, Feb 1-Arr Maria NYork;Jan 26, Ohio, Philadelphia. Cape of Good Hope, Dec 13-Arr bark Merlin, Boston Sept 28, Gibraltar, Jan 26, Air Mary Dale, Philadelphia, Liverpool Feb 1-Arr Patrick Henry, Delano, Washington, Page and Waterloo, NYork.*

From the Boston telegraph office, there was news about the prices of other commodities like coffee, corn, bacon, and lard. The price of Indian corn had dropped sixpence for yellow corn and one shilling and sixpence for white corn. Flour prices were dropping too due to lack of demand. The frost had gone, and continental ports were shipping.

The ships that made it to the eastern seaboard carried news that was old, from one week to many months. It was frustrating for those in the news game.

The NYAP claimed to represent the people—the public interest—in its pursuit of the foreign news. For years, the focus of the telegraphic news remained controlling access to the news from Europe. In reality, the news agency represented the combined resources of six wealthy and powerful institutions. Craig found the agency to be disjointed in every way, with no real system.

Jones was clearly run ragged trying to please the six masters on his own. He was grateful when Craig arrived and they could share the heavy load. He complained that even on stormy nights in winter, when errand boys in Jersey City fell ill or did not show up for work, he himself had to go over to the telegraph terminus in New Jersey, collect the messages waiting there, and return to Manhattan across the Hudson River.

Craig knew from the start that it was inevitable that he too would be called into duty and would experience firsthand the trials Jones had incurred. Of course, when it happened, there was a blizzard raging, adding to the challenge of the late-night assignment.

It was around midnight and Craig started out for the telegraph office at a brisk pace—really the only speed he knew. There was not another soul in sight. A bracing northeasterly wind burned his skin, his eyes watered, and the sleet cut his face. His heavy overcoat slowed him down.

It wasn't the first time a storm had tried to interfere with his plans. He had rowed in all weathers, and stood on rooftops with birds at the ready. Now he was on foot and could only move as fast as his feet would carry him.

He and Helena had chosen to live in New Jersey in the Monmouth area near the coast and near the telegraph station. As always, his instincts were to be physically close to the location of the receipt of news. Tonight he was grateful for his common sense.

As he opened the door, a gust of wind blew in with him and startled the lonely operator who at that moment had nodded off.

"Good evening, sorry to disturb at this late hour. I'm here for the NYAP packet of news."

"No trouble at all. I've been waiting for the young lad who usually comes by much earlier."

"I'm Daniel Craig. The weather seems to have interfered, and I live so close to you I thought I would step in."

The operator handed Craig a thin stack of telegraph messages.

"Not much came in, to be truthful. Must be the weather."

"You're probably right. Only a fool like me would be out on such a night, but duty calls."

"Will you be going across the Hudson tonight?"

As Craig stuffed the news into his inner jacket pocket, he tipped his hat and replied with a sardonic grin, "It's always an adventure chasing the news, isn't it? Good night to you and thank you for your service."

It was cold and miserable but the challenge of getting the news to the NYAP offices seemed to be igniting the intensity that organically drove him to beat all others. When required to compete at that level, he always rose to the occasion and succeeded.

As he jumped aboard the boat ferrying people from New Jersey across the Hudson to Lower Manhattan, he was reminded of his rowing days. He wasn't the only one driven to work long hours in pursuit of an informed society. The telegraph operator and the ferryman were both still up and doing their jobs.

The final step in Craig's midnight run for news, he practically sprinted the few blocks east to the NYAP building and forced himself up the four flights of stairs.

Yawning and rubbing his eyes, he sat at the telegraph table and set to work sending off the news he had collected. There was the usual information about ship arrivals and departures, critical to the many involved in trade along the Eastern Seaboard. Nothing new had arrived on the market price of cotton, or for any commodity, for that matter.

It was a slow night, and it was no surprise to him that not much of interest had moved along the wires. He didn't mind. News was not always exciting or interesting. Yet so much information the NYAP shared was key to people's lives—economically, politically, and personally.

The season of winter slowed down the distribution of news from England and Europe. Fewer ships travelled the North Atlantic at that dark and dangerous time of year. But he believed that if he had not gone to retrieve the latest messages at the telegraph that night, something terribly consequential might have been delayed from the public's knowledge.

His final dispatch of the night was about Irish immigration, although there was not much new in the telegraph report's headline.

Five years later and Potato Famine is still driving the Irish out of Ireland.

The United States had received hundreds of thousands of immigrants since 1845. It was a topic frequently speeding across the telegraph lines. They were arriving at a good time, when great industrial expansion translated into real opportunities for work and a better life in America.

As Craig closed the door and walked down the dark stairway, he started to feel sleepy. The storm had passed and outside in the fresh night air, he took a few deep breaths as he listened to the stillness of the city, normally so noisy and boisterous. He shook off any thoughts about the plight of the Irish and felt a sense of accomplishment. It had always been true for him that the harder the chase, the more he enjoyed the work of journalism.

Thankfully the ferry boat was still running across the Hudson. After a slow and determined walk to his residence, he slipped into bed next to Helena.

"How was it?" she mumbled without opening her eyes.

"Actually, it was a bit of fun, but I wouldn't want to do it all the time. The weather was fierce tonight." Craig looked at Helena, who was fast asleep again. He pulled up the blankets to cover his shivering body and with a smile closed his eyes, satisfied he had done a good job.

The next day, Craig was up early and out the door before first light. He had only managed a few hours' sleep, and the smile turned to a frown. He had already forgotten the enjoyable parts of chasing the news in a blizzard.

A sleep-deprived Craig met a haggard Jones in front of the NYAP offices. The two men trudged forward in the snow that had fallen overnight, nodding to one another, and entered the building. The younger man took the stairs first and asked how things had gone the day before.

"I am going over to Bennett's offices this morning to discuss the situation," Craig declared. "It's unacceptable for men of our quality and experience to have to work such ridiculous hours and in such conditions. It's untenable."

Jones nodded his head but said little.

Craig continued, "Is this a professional news agency or an amateur one? That's what Bennett and his thrifty men must decide."

He removed his watch from the inner pocket of his suit, noting the time. It was too early to visit his boss, so he sat down and got to work alongside Jones. The two men worked diligently, receiving and passing on messages for some time. Nothing of import had been telegraphed yet.

Craig paused and removed his watch. He was impatient and not as focused as he usually was. The clock showed it was 8:30, prompting the newsman to push his chair back from the table.

Without another word, he threw on his winter coat, buttoning it as he rushed to the door. He nodded at Jones as he left the office.

The *Herald* offices were not far. He walked out the Liberty Street entrance across Broadway and after one block, turned left on Nassau Street, walking north to Fulton.

Bennett smiled with surprise at Craig's appearance at his door, squinting at the sunlight infusing his office. It was a typical cold but bright day.

The two men respected each other in the way that competitors in any kind of race appreciate the skills and talents of the other. Regardless of who wins the competition, playing your best always resulted in a successful outcome. Craig thought Bennett would readily agree with him on the steps needed to improve the working conditions at the novel newswire service. But Bennett was a Scot, and he fit the frugal stereotype. The truth was that all the men on the NYAP board were tightfisted.

"How can we provide the best news if we have a shortage of financial means? We need more staff, plain and simple," Craig said.

"I wish we could hire more people. I really do. But where will the money come from?" Bennett said.

Craig was annoyed. The *Herald* was the most successful newspaper of that day. Popular and profitable. Within a decade of its founding in 1835, Bennett had a circulation of 12,000 subscribers, beating out *The Sun* and other newspapers. And still the fifty-five-year-old editor was wary of spending money to invest in the NYAP. Perhaps his age influenced his thinking at the time. He had already fought and won the newspaper game as far as he was concerned.

Craig, in contrast, was still ambitious and at the beginning of creating his own legacy: the first newswire agency serving many news masters. He was not about to give up, as he was just getting started. He realized he had been mistaken in believing that all capitalists knew they had to invest money to generate profits.

"In my opinion, the NYAP should aim higher than merely saving you six a few dollars. We need to hire reporters at every important city along the telegraph network and pay them well. Otherwise, news will remain inconsistent in its quality."

The *Herald*'s owner did not say no. However, he did not say yes either. He was Craig's strongest ally, though only barely. "We will have to bring it to the board," he said.

Craig stood up and shook Bennett's hand. He left trusting that changes would be made in the near future. It was common sense as far as he was concerned.

But months passed, and no board meeting was scheduled.

Then a surprising event occurred that would change the destiny of the newswire service and the man who was most driven to make it succeed.

In May of 1851, Jones arrived at work, solemn and more tired than usual. On this fine spring morning, he broke his routine and did not remove his coat. Instead, he walked toward Craig and handed him a piece of paper, without a word.

Craig looked down at the letter, but before he could read anything, Jones announced, "I am submitting notice of my resignation."

"Are you sure?" Craig said. The paper crumpled slightly in his hand.

"Yes. It's too much for me, Daniel," Jones admitted, uncharacteristically using his colleague's first name. "And the board has made it clear it's in no hurry to hire more staff as you proposed."

"Dear Jones, I understand. The directors don't care how many long hours we work, as long as they get their news."

Jones nodded. "It's up to you now. I did my best with the limited resources I had."

He and Craig shook hands.

Jones left the office for the final time and walked to Bennett's office to submit the now creased letter. As soon as Jones was gone from the *Herald* building, Bennett sent out notes to the entire board of directors to meet at his office. Losing Jones presented a challenge, but it was one that turned out to be easily overcome. Craig was the obvious choice to replace Jones. He was younger, with seemingly boundless energy. He was a hard worker by nature and showed potential for genius. The directors voted on the plan, landing on full support from all.

The next morning, Bennett walked from his office south on Nassau, turned right onto Liberty, and crossed Broadway, arriving early at the NYAP headquarters. Craig was already in place, working the telegraph. He stopped what he was doing when Bennett came through the doorway to offer him the position of general manager for the NYAP.

After hammering out key details of the contract, such as salary and responsibilities, Bennett held out his hand to seal the deal. The deal fell easily into place because everyone had been thinking for a while that Craig was capable of managing the operation. With Jones taking himself out of the picture, it was the obvious next move for the NYAP.

Craig immediately showed he would be pushing the directors to invest more money in the fledgling operation.

"James, I happily take on the work, but as I have already told you, we need more resources to do a proper job."

His own ambitions coincided with the business goals of the men funding the unprecedented growth of a new era in communications as more and more cities and towns were being connected by the telegraph. That guaranteed growth for the NYAP, but only if they could sustainably manage the flow of information.

The hard-bitten Yankee immediately set to work putting down on paper his vision for newsgathering under his leadership at the NYAP. It would be a blueprint for a novel approach to news and would be practised by the NYAP staff going forward: News reporting using the objective voice as opposed to the subjective, opinion style in the newspapers of the day. Information would be fact-based and gathered from reliable and credible sources.

Just as Craig was transitioning to his new role as GM, a brand-new newspaper joined the NYAP: *The New York Times*. It was founded by two men who had worked for Greeley at the *New-York Tribune* as editors, Henry Jarvis Raymond and George Jones.

There were now seven masters on the board of directors, whom Craig had to convince to enshrine his ideas into the NYAP's policies and the required professional practices of journalists they hired.

Chapter 8
Fighting for Quality Reporters

Craig was working long hours, often seven days a week, diligently and some might say, feverishly, creating a news network that would stretch across the continent and beyond.

In his campaign to grow a nationwide systematic newswire service, Craig spoke to whomever would listen, including government officials farther north. In a letter to Nova Scotia's Pictou County representative George R. Young, he wrote:

> *The public have come to regard all telegraphic newspaper despatches with suspicion or disgust. I beg to state to you, very briefly, the leading features of the news arrangements which I am now making on behalf of the New York Associated Press.*

Craig didn't mince words about his opinion of the telegraph news, saying it came through in

> *fits and starts, often hazily, often lazily, usually in third- or fourth-hand reports often obscured by the prejudices of partisans.*

He said his goal was to improve the existing inefficient and irresponsible system of news gathering and distribution, and he outlined how that would be achieved by the AP.

> *It would cover all important news—as well that relating to commerce as to general events—the wish being to raise the standard of telegraphic reports, both as regards the matter and the manner of the same—to make them what they ought to be; reliable for accuracy, and the medium through which all really important or decidedly interesting news shall be placed before the public, with the utmost despatch.*

Craig envisioned a news agency that would be the first of its kind. Under his leadership, the New York Associated Press would expand to distribute news beyond the city of New York. He intended to sell the NYAP news to any newspaper on the continent.

The relentless newsman was aware his plans were ambitious, and that some might call him driven. He did not mind. He had a clear vision.

He also had little patience for mediocre work, and scolded telegraph operators who didn't live up to his expectations. He often complained about the unreliable nature of the telegraph news to Helena, "Most telegraph operators are not skilled enough to be called news correspondents. Many have no background as writers. They are translators of Morse code."

To his former colleague Jones, he often proposed, "We need our own staff to do the writing. That way we can rely on it being fact-based."

Some operators embellished news coming through on the wire as they passed it along. The regular practice at the time was for a telegraph operator in one city to telegraph only a few lines summarizing the main facts about an event. The editor on the receiving end then had to use their imagination to turn these lines into a story of several hundred words.

Craig cracked down on the practice, sending out a telegraph to operators with strict instructions that if a story was important enough that details were justified, those details were also worth the wire costs.

An experienced telegraph reporter rebutted, "Editors do not know the difference between real and imaginary news."

That disrespectful attitude was exactly the opposite of what Craig demanded in his journalism. For him, accuracy had become an issue. Reliability had also become an issue, and the NYAP's credibility was at stake.

Craig knew, in his heart, the whole journalistic venture would fail without good men to chase, gather, and write the news. Before he could hire any staff, he had the burden of proving to the board of directors the company could pay those salaries. He knew his plan to expand the wire service would depend upon how many newspapers he could include in this arrangement.

So, he planned an ambitious tour of fourteen cities in the United States and British North America, as Canada was not yet formed as a nation.

Helena and the children, Ida and William, saw him off. They waved as the train sped away, heading off on what promised to be an exhausting journey, which was why she had decided not to accompany him with two little ones. They had shared many adventures from Baltimore to Boston and Halifax, but this one he would take on his own.

Craig spent a gruelling number of weeks travelling and meeting with news editors and publishers in Boston, Halifax,

Albany, Buffalo, Detroit, Cincinnati, Louisville, St. Louis, Charleston, Richmond, Norfolk, Mobile, New Orleans, Baltimore, and Philadelphia.

Generally, Craig had found more agreement than disagreement among the newsmen he had met with. The conversations were long and involved as one would expect with a new operation or service, but negotiations weren't difficult. There seemed to be a general consensus on the inherent value of receiving a package of news from the NYAP that was based on factual information and not opinion.

In Baltimore, nearing the end of the lengthy tour, the new managing editor of the NYAP was reunited with his old mentor and boss Arunah S. Abell, still managing *The Sun* to great success. The two men shook hands as they smiled warmly at one another.

"Congratulations, Daniel, managing the New York Associated Press! Not bad. Not bad at all."

"Thank you."

"I always suspected New York was where you would land."

"Kind of you to say. Helena said the same thing. She sends her regards."

"How are she and the children?"

"Doing well. Thanks for asking. And your family?"

"Yes, yes. All is well on that front. Now tell me all about your new job and your travels."

"First I will say I'm enthusiastic about my new role. But honestly the operation is quite a mess, needs major reorganization and some staff, and of course, as always, not nearly enough money."

"Which is why you are here, I presume?"

"Yes. I'm building a clientele outside New York. It's the only way it will survive. Besides which it's natural to grow nationally and internationally."

Abell chuckled, "It is called the New York Associated Press, isn't it?"

"I'll be making it into a national service if I have anything to say about it. All Americans deserve to get the news, not just those in New York. I feel certain most newspapers will be happy to receive the quality of news we're gathering."

"The news on the telegraph isn't always the best, now, is it?"

"Not all telegraph operators are upholding the standards I would prefer. Some are less skilled and don't have the commitment to reliable information that we do in news."

"Oh, I agree with that. So much information is not recorded properly. Some operators pay little attention to details and others like to enrich some dispatches. You can't always rely on it."

Craig thought to himself how quickly the pair had fallen back into their old easy conversational style. It was always inspiring to talk with Abell, perhaps because they so often agreed on matters related to journalism.

"So, I can rely on you to become a committed client for the NYAP? We can discuss the figures later, but right now I am hoping to sign up fourteen newspapers on the continent, as a start."

Abell nodded his head. "I admire your ambitions, my friend. Count me in. *The Sun* will be happy to publish the NYAP news, especially the foreign news. You're still getting the news from the steamships first."

"If we were at Cape Race, Newfoundland, then we would truly be the first to get the news from England. It's thousands of miles farther east than Nova Scotia."

"That's true. But the telegraph hasn't reached Cape Race yet. It could be years before such a remote place gets the telegraph."

"It will happen soon enough, given its key location on the edge of North America. When it does, the NYAP will be there chasing news! I promise you that!"

Abell smiled a knowing smile. "I have no doubt that you will, Daniel."

Craig returned the smiled and handed his old friend a thin booklet as he commented, "I have taken the time to write down my ideas. Sort of a guide for how to practise news reporting in the modern world."

Leafing through it quickly, the *Sun* editor noticed words such as *fact-based news, accuracy, credible sources,* and *reliable information*. These were novel ideas. Reporting was evolving from opinion-based newspapers—the way it had always been done—to fact-based news over the telegraph wires, the revolutionary new technology.

Abell looked up at his colleague with respect. "This is a powerful document. All the right ideas and words to turn journalism into a respectable occupation."

"Arunah, Baltimore is number thirteen on my tour. Only Philadelphia left before I return home, thank goodness. I tell you, it's been astounding to discover how the editors welcomed my ideas."

"If it improves the state of news passing on the telegraph, it will be a worthy development."

Nodding his head, Craig replied, "I can truly say that I have found everywhere only one sentiment, and that is that the general character of telegraphic news is a disgrace to all concerned."

Several weeks later, back at work in New York, Craig prepared for his meeting with the board of directors. He would report to his bosses and request approval for the hiring spree he wanted to carry out.

As the newsmen settled into their chairs, the ever-confident Craig stood at the end of the long wooden table and surveyed his employers.

"Gentlemen, I return with good news."

Bennett from *The Herald* sat to his right, bolstering his confidence. The older man leaned in with interest, as did a couple of others.

"As you know, I travelled to fourteen cities from New Orleans to Halifax. And everywhere I went, I heard similar complaints about the quality of telegraph news."

A murmur spread among the group of editors. They had discussed the problem ad nauseam in the past and all were in agreement on the subject. No one had come up with a solution to it.

Craig then raised his eyebrows and looked around the table. "So, I have returned with contracts to deliver news to fourteen publications, from all the cities I visited."

Bennett and the others tapped their fists lightly on the table and looked pleased.

"You all received a copy of my circular before I left for the tour. I am delighted to say the editors and publishers I met with agreed with the NYAP's approach to news going forward. Actually I was a little surprised with how the general feeling was that news based on facts gathered with an objective mindset is the best approach to take now."

Bennett and Beach looked at each other and then at Hale, pleased that Craig's ideas about a more independent press were resonating with so many newsmen in the country.

"Now they did raise concerns about the New York-focused reports we will be sending out, so I anticipate that will continue to be an issue as we grow. But it's a problem for another day. Today we can feel good. The NYAP is the news service they trust to send them the ever-important foreign news. And I am confident more newspapers will be signing up."

It meant the directors would not have to dig as deep into their own pockets to finance the transition to a more organized journalism service. Craig then moved on to a subject that was crucial for success.

"I seek your approval today to hire fourteen reporters to work for us from all corners of the continent."

Acutely aware of every tapping finger and shuffling foot, he observed several of them crossing their arms and pursing their thin lips. Ignoring their discomfort, he continued, "We thus expect to obtain, from authentic sources, on all the important news of the day, over ten or fifteen thousand miles of telegraph wires, radiating from New York to nearly every city or town of note in the United States or British American provinces."

He assured the board of directors that very particular care would be taken while selecting the correspondents, especially the ones who would be handling important commercial information.

And he repeated his demand for a liberal salary for these special correspondents. This made some of the newspapermen shift in their seats, clearly uncomfortable with talk of more spending up front.

He argued that to succeed, they had to ensure always using the most competent, attentive, and experienced correspondents, as well as the unlimited expenditure of money. He knew he was asking the men to take a risk and invest in an untested service, and he understood that anything new provoked fear in even the most confident men.

But Craig won them over by appealing to their capitalist tendencies. "News over the wires is something brand new in journalism, and the NYAP has so much room to grow, just like what has happened in the telegraph industry. Everywhere you look in this city now, you see telegraph poles and lines."

Craig saw a few of the men nodding in agreement. They had all witnessed the exponential growth since the telegraph launched in 1844. Fortunes were being made by capitalists investing in telegraph poles and glass insulators and anything to do with the telegraph as the communications network expanded in all directions on the continent. Their newspapers were doing well.

The small group of powerful men in the room had to agree that their new managing editor was leading the way, taking the NYAP in the right direction, albeit not the one they had originally envisioned.

Craig continued, "Gentlemen of known capacity, fidelity, and promptness will be located at New Orleans, Mobile, Charleston, Norfolk, Richmond, Washington, Baltimore, Philadelphia, Boston, Albany, Buffalo, Cincinnati, St. Louis, and Detroit."

He added that his vision for the NYAP went beyond the United States. It had always been a North American proposition for him, and staff would also be hired in Toronto, Montreal and Quebec City, Halifax, and Saint John, New Brunswick.

All the news they gathered in each location would be wired directly to the NYAP headquarters on Broadway in the Financial District of Manhattan—some might say the centre of the world.

As with all new commercial ventures, it would mean a financial investment to create the NYAP's national news network, but they could now see that with the knowledge Craig had gathered during his tour, they were encountering a unique opportunity to expand their influence and profits.

After much discussion and consternation around the table about the cost of the plan, the board of directors lifted their hands in a vote, showing support. Within months of taking over from Jones, Craig had demonstrated not only vision and exceptional organizational skills, but also creativity and determination.

Energized, Craig told them, "Gentlemen, my ultimate goal for the AP is the early acquisition of important news, by telegraph, for publication."

With the board's backing, he dived into the hiring process, initially focusing on key locations: the power centres in North America. He took particular care in selecting the NYAP correspondent in Washington, D.C.

Lawrence Gobright was his man, and clearly understood his role as defined by his boss. He would go on to tell a congressional committee: "My business is to communicate facts. My instructions do not allow me to make any comments upon the facts which I communicate. My dispatches are sent to papers of all manner of politics, and the editors say they are able to make their own comments upon the facts which are sent to them."

Gobright promised to confine himself to covering what he considered legitimate news. "I do not act as a politician belonging to any school, but try to be truthful and impartial. My dispatches are a merely dry matter of fact and detail."

In the next couple of years, the NYAP would be transformed. Craig had accomplished much of what he had set out to do in that meeting with the board of directors.

The NYAP correspondents were spread out across the US, Upper and Lower Canada, and the eastern colonies. Their job duties were not so much reporting news as much as summarizing the information received from the steamships and over the telegraph wires.

Craig's view was that his men were correspondents rather than reporters, and it was not their responsibility to be primary news-gatherers. They were there to collate the news flowing through the wires and then transmit it to New York.

However, at strategic geographic points such as Cape Race, Liverpool, and Washington, D.C., NYAP staff were given more freedom and were expected to gather news directly. They could talk to officials and credible sources on the local scene and get the details about events occurring, and write their own news reports to be sent via telegraph to the NYAP.

Craig realized that in small towns or locations of less importance, important news could definitely arise, so he told his NYAP agents to get in touch with local newspaper editors or officials to get the details when something of interest was occurring.

It was a rare occasion to read news that had been uncovered by a reporter with firsthand knowledge. That professional role did not exist yet. So much was occurring as the country rapidly expanded, but few were employed to observe and document it all—the key role of news journalism. It was a new field, driven by the new possibilities offered by the telegraph. Fact-based news told from an objective or neutral viewpoint were new concepts the NYAP wire service was developing as it grew.

A decade before the telegraph was launched in 1844, a desire for a more independent press had begun emerging in the United States. In the first issue of the *New York Herald* in 1835, publisher and editor James Bennett had written:

*We shall support no party—be the agent of no faction
or coterie, and we care nothing for any election, or any
candidate from president down to constable. We shall
endeavour to record facts on every public and proper
subject, stripped of verbiage and colouring.*

Bennett and Craig shared similar values when it came to news, which was partly why their paths had aligned at the NYAP.

Although it had not been the original intention of the founders of the NYAP, they had set in motion a grand experiment in an emerging style of journalism. Six competitors cooperating and, through that collaborative spirit, creating a new, defining principle for covering news events: the objective collection of the facts and reporting of them. They were entrepreneurs after all, and this novel approach to news had the potential to translate into major profits for them all. As the NYAP developed and expanded under Craig's leadership, the concept of objectivity in journalism came into focus as the cornerstone of news reporting.

In those foundational years for journalism, the city of New York itself was in the throes of a construction project of its own, this one aimed at displaying the superior prowess of America over England.

The World Fair would open in 1853, and the newly constructed Crystal Palace would be the centrepiece, displaying all of the inventions and breakthroughs Americans were responsible for in the march toward progress.

The American Exhibition space openly copied London's Crystal Palace, which had been built two years earlier and was admired and lauded by all. The site chosen was a four-acre piece of land between 40th and 42nd streets, in what would later become Bryant Park in Midtown Manhattan.

Once the New York version was constructed, the iron and glass building was described as one of the finest buildings in the world and Americans patted themselves on the backs for going further than London had.

President Abraham Lincoln summed up public sentiment of the time when he wrote that the great difference between Young America and Old Fogy England was the number of inventions, discoveries, and innovations.

Walt Whitman, a young poet living in Brooklyn, would write in an 1857 edition of the *Brooklyn Daily Times* that Crystal Palace was

unsurpassed anywhere for beauty.

A young Samuel Clemens, who was not yet Mark Twain, wrote in a letter to his sister Pamela that it was

a perfect fairy palace.

Patriotic hearts swelled, and more than a million people visited the exhibition.

Like all New Yorkers, Craig and Helena were eager to view Crystal Palace, a testament to America's genius, and they were impressed by the grandeur of the place.

One of the most attention-grabbing inventions came from Elisha Otis: an elevator. Never seen before, installed centre stage under the stunning dome of the building: The Otis elevator—a platform riding between four vertical rails—was too tall to place anywhere else.

The Craigs stood before the exhibit, observing the inventor himself riding up and down the elevator, occasionally cutting the rope by which it was supported, and appearing to fall. Otis's innovation protected him: It was a sort of automatic emergency brake that, if the lifting cable broke, would prevent the platform or car from falling. His daring stunt could be seen by everyone. What few at the time could foresee was the impact his invention would have on high-rise buildings.

As he watched the demonstration over and over again, Craig wondered aloud, "When can I get one of these for the NYAP building? How marvellous it would be to avoid those four flights of steps every day."

Helena smiled. She had been listening to her husband's complaints about those stairs for years. "It will save a lot of energy. How ingenious," she said.

Another invention attracting attention at Crystal Palace was Isaac Singer's sewing machine, which would end up in practically every American home in the following few years. The enduring Mason jar was also created during this period.

The invention of the electric telegraph was not a highlight at the New York Exhibition, as it had been engineered a decade earlier. And the transatlantic telegraph was still only an idea in the minds of a few pioneers.

Still, the innovation of the telegraph had itself sparked new industries and a manufacturing bonanza with dozens of factories being constructed in New York and Brooklyn. They produced the telegraph key sets and the wire cables for the telegraph network to expand across the continent. And other telegraph-related equipment was created, such as the glass insulator. It was a small, dome-shaped glass which covered the wire where it connected to the top of the wooden telegraph pole. It protected the wire, with electricity coursing through it, from rain and the elements. Millions of the dome-shaped glass insulators were produced at factories in New York and Brooklyn and sold throughout North America as it became a wired continent. But the story of the telegraph and its revolution was not over. Americans had conquered the land but not the sea.

Chapter 9
Continental Connections

Wall Street was around the corner from the NYAP offices in the centre of the Financial District in Lower Manhattan. The Merchants' Exchange stood proudly in an oversized building in a Greek Revival style; an eighty-foot-wide dome topped the facade of gigantic Italian marble columns. A stately presence amidst the noise and clamour of the growing city, it was where the New York Stock Exchange lived and men of commerce met to negotiate the business of trade. It is where investments were being made during this period of rapid industrial expansion and so it was a natural place for Craig to run into an old colleague from his Halifax days.

As he strolled along Wall Street during a break from the unending work at the NYAP, he saw a familiar face walking toward him. Frederic Newton Gisborne was an Englishman who had left his homeland and had quickly distinguished himself in the telegraph industry on this side of the Atlantic, first as chief operator for the Montreal Telegraph Company and then as superintendent of the Nova Scotia Telegraph.

The two men had not seen one another since their days in Halifax, five years before.

Gisborne smiled widely as he approached Craig. They shook hands.

"What a pleasant surprise to see you here, Daniel," Gisborne said. "I was hoping I might."

"Delighted to see you again, Frederic."

"I had heard you were now running the New York Associated Press. Congratulations. Not a little job you've taken on."

"It's a disorganized mess, but I'm doing what I can to manage the growth. So what brings you to my fair city?"

"I'm looking for investors to lay a telegraph line across the island of Newfoundland."

Craig raised his eyebrows. "I see." He had been investing some of his own money in the expanding new technology and was looking for more opportunities to earn profits. "Newfoundland is closest to Europe, so I left Halifax for St. John's and have been working with the government there, as they are deeply interested in bringing the telegraph to the island."

"This is excellent news to receive today."

"Daniel, after being in Quebec and then Nova Scotia, I realized that if we are ever to connect the continents via a submarine telegraph cable, it would have to be landed in the most easterly point in North America."

"So you're hoping that we'll have a cable under the Atlantic Ocean someday? I agree. It seems only natural that the telegraph will go beyond land communication." "Indeed. First, though, the telegraph must be built across Cabot Strait, connecting Newfoundland to the North American continent. And then across the land from west to east on the island itself."

"It is the closest land mass to Ireland."

Gisborne nodded. "In 1850, I signed a contract with the Newfoundland government to build a telegraph network across the island from the capital city of St. John's to Port Aux Basques, a small fishing village on the west coast."

"I always wanted to get over to Newfoundland but I never made it, so I'm curious." Craig motioned to a bench off the side of the walkway. "Shall we sit down? Do you have time? I want to know everything."

Although he was interested from an investing point of view, he knew he had stumbled onto an exciting development in the telegraph story that he would later write and share over the wires.

The two of them sat down, removing their hats as they turned toward each other in an effort to tune out the buzz emanating from the dozens of men in top hats having similar conversations as they walked in and out of the Merchant Exchange.

Gisborne continued, "Newfoundland stretches about 320 miles from west to east. Most of its people live in small bays and coves all around the coastline. There are no roads. Boats provide transportation to and from the capital for supplies. The land is rocky, boggy, and forested, and goes on for hundreds of miles."

"How on earth did you tame the wilderness?"

"Well, actually, that's why I'm here. I failed. The crews I hired were only able to create an fifty-five-mile bridle path from St. John's to Brigus, Conception Bay. Clearing the land became impossible. And I ran out of money."

Craig was sympathetic and patted him on the shoulder. "Well, I'm sure you'll succeed. I admire you for taking it on. Now you need more men to believe in it. I personally do not doubt that you'll find what you need here. Everyone is out to make a fortune on the telegraph."

"I'm determined to get a telegraph line through that corner of North America. You know, my proposal includes stationing the boat *Wanderer* at Cape Race," Gisborne said.

Craig's eyes lit up. Cape Race intrigued him because he knew it was where he and the NYAP could get first access to foreign news. While living in Halifax, Craig had learned about the remote headland, six hundred miles farther east, ever closer to England and Europe. Cape Race was well known to mariners, and on maps since the fifteenth century—an important place on the great trade circle between England and the United States.

Rugged and stark, Cape Race was all sharp cliff edges and open sky. It was known as the ironbound coast because of its charcoal cliffs rising to the height of 100 feet or more. The jagged shoreline of reefs and shoals—a foggy mirage—sat waiting for ships to wreck.

The largest, closest community were a half-dozen Irish Catholic families in Portugal Cove South, about twelve miles from the headland. There were frequent calls for a light to be placed at the cape to protect ships from slamming into the cliffs.

But Craig had never been there. Cape Race had become a mythical place in his mind, a meeting place between the old and new worlds.

He could see that Newfoundland, an island located between those worlds, was destined to play a key role in the transatlantic telegraph cable project. Sitting on the edge of the continent, closest to Ireland, it was the fastest route for the transmission of important news. He vowed to ensure the NYAP would have a presence at Cape Race as soon as it was humanly possible.

A few days later, Craig was out for his usual walk to get some fresh air while observing the expanding world around him. Today he had chosen to walk south along Broadway, noticing the social activity at the many Paris-style cafes with French names which now occupied the grand avenue. It was an unusually warm day for winter, and New Yorkers were out enjoying the afternoon sun.

He liked walking through the Battery at the tip of the island, gazing at the ocean, examining the steamships anchored there waiting to unload their cargo.

As he turned around to head north and return to work, Craig scanned the crowd and was not surprised to see it filled with serious men in formal suits—men of commerce—talking about the latest inventions and the progress being made in the city and country.

He spied Cyrus W. Field, a rich retired businessman, chatting with inventor Samuel F.B. Morse. Field was a self-made millionaire in the business of paper production and sales.

The curious newsman, always on the hunt for new information and developments in the city, suspected something significant was afoot. He was unable to control his questioning nature. He walked slowly toward them, politely holding back until the conversation ended. Neither seemed aware of Craig's presence.

The inventor tipped his hat, as did Field, as they began to walk off in opposite directions.

Craig seized the opportunity and moved quickly.

"Good day, Mr. Field. How are you on this fine day?"

Slightly startled, Field turned and upon recognizing Craig, held out his hand.

"Good morning, Mr. Craig."

Craig got right to the point. "I couldn't help but notice you and Mr. Morse having an intense conversation. What are you two up to now?"

"Well, if you must know, we were speaking about the transatlantic telegraph cable. I have been in discussions with a man from England named Frederic Gisborne, who had been working on the Newfoundland line," Field shared excitedly.

Craig replied, "I just ran into him recently; he's looking for investors for the telegraph in Newfoundland."

Field nodded his head. "The job is more monumental and costly than he or anyone anticipated. The poor man has lost everything trying to build the line on that godforsaken island. The interior is completely untamed, thousands of miles of nothing but trees, rocks, and bogs."

Craig frowned. "Am I right to surmise, he has convinced you to get involved?"

"Yes, foolish as it may be, I am intrigued. I have done some research, and I have decided to invest."

"It's an ambitious endeavour, but I personally believe it can be engineered. It would be, no doubt, of great benefit to civilization," Craig said.

"If you are interested in investing, I'm hosting a meeting at my house tomorrow night at seven to discuss the entire project."

"Gramercy Park, right? I'll be there. But to be honest, I'm interested in how this could benefit the NYAP. This could change the world."

Field nodded in agreement. "Out of self-interest, I invite you to attend the gathering. Letting the world know what we are doing could bring support from other investors and governments."

They bid each other good day, and Craig picked up his pace as he returned to work, buoyed by the news tip he had stumbled upon.

The next evening, Craig made his way to the east side of the island of Manhattan, to Gramercy Park, where Field lived. The residential neighbourhood included a two-acre private park for the enjoyment of the people residing in the mansions and brownstones built on the four sides of the square, replicating the residential squares in London.

The boss of the NYAP removed his overcoat and was led through a well-appointed sitting room with tall windows enhanced by green velvet curtains framing French provincial furniture. Craig wasn't at all surprised by the poshness of the place. Gramercy Park was where men with financial security lived: men who could seriously consider investing in a project of the magnitude of an oceanic communications system. As Craig entered a study and library filled with bookshelves, he could see Field standing behind his wooden desk.

The potential investors crowded around the desk, some seated in hard-back chairs and others standing as they all focused on the maps and charts laid out.

Field's neighbour Peter Cooper was there: a highly respected capitalist who had started out as a working man's son and was known for his noble tendencies and the heart of a prince. He was an industrialist who had retired with a large fortune from a number of ventures, including manufacturing the first steam-powered railroad locomotive engine, called the *Tom Thumb*. Cooper did not need the money he might earn from investing in the transatlantic telegraph, but he had been convinced by Field that connecting the continents was a worthy effort and would be of great benefit to the public.

Craig nodded his head at Field and Cooper. They were involved in an intense discussion, and he didn't want to interrupt so he found a spot to stand against one of the shelves, most comfortable as a neutral observer. From his standpoint, he could record important developments mentally; a notebook would attract too much attention.

It had been years since he had done any actual news gathering in the field. But he was keenly interested in the outcome of tonight's meeting. He noticed that Morse, the inventor of the land telegraph, was also in attendance, as well as Moses Taylor, Marshall O. Roberts, and Chandler White. Not surprisingly, Frederic Gisborne, the man who currently owned the contract with the Newfoundland government, was also there.

Field picked up a piece of correspondence several pages in length and looked around at the entrepreneurs dressed in tailored suits with coiffed hair seated before him. He launched into his final pitch for investments in the transatlantic telegraph project.

"Well, gentlemen, thank you all for coming tonight. This will be our final discussion. Time for decisions."

For the previous three nights, they had gathered to discuss the details of the mammoth project being proposed by Field and his brother, David Dudley Field Jr., a lawyer and enthusiastic supporter of his sibling's instincts.

They had also discussed the costs of the project, which they knew many people believed was impossible. The fact that they had all returned to Field's house this evening proved they were more than interested.

Admitting he was neither a scientist nor an engineer, Field told them he had saved some important information for their final meeting.

"At the bottom of the North Atlantic Ocean lies a plateau, and it is a perfect place to safely lay a thin telegraph cable!" Field said with excitement.

Samuel F.B. Morse quickly added in a serious tone, "It's called Maury's Plateau, after the man who discovered it."

Field continued, "Gentlemen, immediately after being approached by Mr. Gisborne about investing in this challenge, I wrote to the Naval Observatory in Washington to determine whether it was possible. I received this letter signed by the Secretary of the US Navy, the Honourable J.C. Dobbin, and a Lieutenant Matthew Maury."

Craig was not aware of the results of the ocean survey, so he leaned in, curious to know more. Field surveyed the faces of the men gathered before him, now lit up.

"Last summer, they conducted research concerning the winds and currents of the North Atlantic and completed a series of soundings, from the shores of Newfoundland to Ireland." He lifted the letter so he could read out the next paragraph, about the plateau, for extra emphasis.

"It is neither too deep nor too shallow; yet it is so deep that the wires, once landed, will remain forever beyond the reach of vessels' anchors, icebergs, and drifts of any kind, and so shallow that the wires may be readily lodged upon the bottom."

The extraordinary news prompted some men to hit the desks with their fists and others to bounce out of their chairs as they all looked at one another, absorbing the information. It boosted their confidence in the project.

Field kept the meeting focused by walking to a five-foot-tall globe and pointing to the eastern edge of the island of Newfoundland. Then he traced his index finger slowly across the map of the world to the western edge of the island of Ireland. His audience followed his finger as it travelled the distance between the two islands on either side of the North Atlantic.

"These two points offer the shortest distance across the Atlantic to lay a cable connecting the continents. The distance between the nearest points is about 1,550 miles."

Cooper moved forward and placed his finger on Newfoundland, while Field held his on Ireland. The two men stood face to face, symbolizing the close connections they imagined would materialize because of the transatlantic cable. Field and Cooper grinned, and the group erupted in laughter.

Moments later Cooper dampened the mood; he verbalized what many were thinking, as they returned to their seats. "It sounds like an incredible opportunity but also an expensive one. How much will it cost, do you imagine?"

Field replied, "I intend to create a budget outlining the project's expenses. It goes without saying this will be expensive. But if we can communicate across the vast Atlantic, life as we know it will be altered, for the betterment of humankind. That is where the real value lies."

Cooper was the first to stand up and announce that he would invest a substantial sum of money in the project. The others applauded and were quick to assure Field they, too, would be investing.

The first step in the project would be to connect the island of Newfoundland with Cape Breton, Nova Scotia and the mainland of North America. Laying the cable under Cabot Strait was the first challenge to overcome. A cable already existed between England and France, which had proved that submarine telegraph lines could work.

Once the island was connected with the mainland, the next step would be completing the telegraph network across Newfoundland to its eastern edge.

Field's brother David then stepped forward as the lawyer in the room, and began formal proceedings. The group voted in favour of forming the New York, Newfoundland and London Telegraph Company, reflecting the geographic triangle involved in the cable project.

Initially, Cooper and Field, along with Moses Taylor, Chandler White, and Marshall O. Roberts, invested 500,000 pounds sterling—Newfoundland's currency at the time—in the international venture. Cooper made the largest financial investment in the transatlantic telegraph cable project, which was probably why he was voted in as president of the company. Field became vice president. Taylor was treasurer, and they were all directors of the company, along with Roberts and White.

Morse was director with the title of electrician. The man at the centre of the land telegraph invention was now being delegated a supporting act in the ocean telegraph.

Craig concluded he had enough information to write a decent story. He was happy to have exclusive access to what was happening.

As he made his way to the door, he offered a nod of thanks to Field, who was engaged in the conversation. He also made eye contact with Gisborne, a man he admired for his dedication to this new technology. Who had lost everything in trying to build the Newfoundland telegraph. He had even been jailed in St. John's briefly, after labourers working for his company surrounded his office, demanding their pay. But he was broke and had been forced to declare bankruptcy.

Now Gisborne's Electric-Telegraph Company and its contract with the Newfoundland government would be bought out by the New York, Newfoundland and London Telegraph company. Another land-telegraph pioneer would be relegated to a supportive role in the submarine technology.

After raising substantial venture capital in New York, Field boarded a steamer to travel to Newfoundland to meet with the island's colonial governor, Sir Charles Henry Darling, about the company's plans.

He negotiated for more money to support the construction of the telegraph network across the massive island. The Newfoundland government contributed 500,000 US dollars up front and 500,000 more at the completion of the project.

Buoyed by the success of his visit to St. John's, Field travelled to London, seeking more investors and knowledge from scientific and engineering minds who were focusing on submarine telegraphy in Europe.

At the NYAP headquarters in Lower Manhattan, Craig kept up with the activities of the company, occasionally sending brief notes to Field. So far, it seemed it was full steam ahead. He was aware that Field was in England purchasing the actual cable for the link between mainland North America and the island of Newfoundland.

Craig glanced at the newspaper on his desk and read the latest disturbing headline:

The SS Arctic Sinks Killing more than 300 People.

The massive vessel sank fifty miles south of Cape Race. It had happened two weeks before, but news of the tragedy had only just arrived.

Shaking his head, Craig muttered, "Damn that North Atlantic." He could not wait for the day when the continents were linked by the telegraph and the chase for connection across the ocean would end.

Chapter 10
The Transatlantic Telegraph

It was a year later, on August 15th, and sixty people were on board the steamer the *James Adger*, leaving New York behind as they travelled to an island they knew only as remote and foggy with plenty of codfish. As they departed from the Brooklyn wharf, there were cheers and shouts from the hundreds of people who shared in the excitement surrounding the transatlantic telegraph project. The directors of the New York, Newfoundland and London Telegraph Company. and their families were setting off on a challenging expedition, connecting Newfoundland to the North American continent.

The man leading the way, Cyrus W. Field, intended to bring his investors to the west coast of Newfoundland to observe the laying of the telegraph cable across Cabot Strait: 85 miles from Cape Ray, near Port Aux Basques, to Aspy Bay, Cape Breton.

On the deck stood Field, Cooper, Morse, Taylor, Roberts, and White and their wives and families. Everyone waved gleefully at the crowds on the docks.

The *Sarah L. Bryant* was on her way to Port Aux Basques from England, transporting the cable. The barque also carried the crew who would lay the telegraph wire from Cape Ray to Nova Scotia.

Field had invited a man named John Mullaly to document the entire excursion. The writer was tasked with writing a book, which he would title *A Trip to Newfoundland*. He would submit a shortened version to the popular *Harper's New Monthly Magazine*.

Their first break from the tumultuous Atlantic waters came when the ship docked at Halifax, Nova Scotia, en route to Newfoundland. The passengers on board the steamer noted a stark contrast to the way they were greeted compared with the noisy farewell they had experienced at home in New York.

About one hundred locals were assembled on the wharf but they gazed at the newcomers with, as Mullaly would write, the *most listless curiosity*, and the New Yorkers had a sense that everything seemed to be a *half a century behind the age*. Describing the city of Halifax itself, he would write that it had a

most desolate, woebegone aspect and looked as if two thirds
of its inhabitants were asleep.

They stepped off the ship and were off exploring and investigating the colonial city, like true Yankees. Unfortunately, an unpleasant encounter occurred when an inflexible hotel manager refused to alter his routine and provide a meal to the hungry group. Mullaly would write,

We left in disgust and with a hearty wish that we were
in New York again.

The next port of call after Halifax was Port Aux Basques, on the western tip of Newfoundland. But when they arrived, Field was informed that the cable had not yet arrived from England. Until it did, the directors decided to continue steaming east to the capital, St. John's.

As the *James Adger* passed by Cape Race, at the southeast corner of the island, it kept a good distance from the coastline of charcoal cliffs. Out on deck, some of the company directors stood side by side and studied the infamous headland, known for centuries for its deadly waters.

"There will be a lighthouse at Cape Race next year," Chandler White predicted. He had written to the government of Newfoundland about the need for a beacon to be placed at the southeast tip of the island:

> *Cape Race is the point on the great highway of nations, toward which every mariner bound on either the eastern or western voyage, between Europe and America, looks as to a place of departure. It being nearly in the line of the great circle-sailing, between the ports of Liverpool, London, and Havre, on the one side of the Atlantic, and Boston, New York, and Philadelphia on the other.*

"And we will have a telegraph line going in there at the same time," Field chimed in. "I don't know if I mentioned this, but as soon as we can get the telegraph through Cape Race and Trepassey, Daniel Craig intends to put a news boat here for the NYAP to chase the news arriving from Europe."

The *James Adger* changed to a northerly direction until it reached the hidden harbour of St. John's. After a weeklong voyage at sea, the vessel moved slowly, gliding through the narrows, a slim entryway into one of the deepest harbours in the world.

The New Yorkers were impressed by towering hills surrounding the town. Despite the rain, the Yankees commented on the stunning scenery and rugged beauty of the area.

St. John's was the capital of one of Britain's oldest colonies and geographically, the closest land to the old world. In 1497, John Cabot claimed it for England.

About 120,000 people were now allowed to settle and live in the colony of Newfoundland year-round. For much of the previous three centuries, England had only allowed fishermen and workers from the British Isles and Europe to travel to Newfoundland to work for six to seven months of the year on the cod fishery. It was seasonal employment, and when weather prevented any work on the sea, the fishermen were sent back home to their homelands until the next season began.

Eventually though, more and more of the temporary foreign workers refused to leave. They had made business and personal relationships while on the island and they wanted to settle. Ultimately, the monarchy was forced to let go of control and allow settlement.

Tiny outports developed all along the coastline of the island, with a half dozen families creating a new community around a sustainable inshore fishing life. Still, in 1855, most people on the island lived in St. John's near the harbour, where trade and commerce were concentrated along Water and Duckworth streets.

As the *James Adger* steamed at a snail's pace toward King's Wharf, the main landing on the northeastern side of the harbour, the New Yorkers were impressed with how crowded it was with steamships, fishing boats, and sailboats. There were dozens of vessels from many different places: England, France, Spain, Portugal, and the Caribbean.

Along the waterfront, slender wharves jutted out like fingers, covered with salted codfish being loaded into barrels for export to Jamaica in exchange for rum. Essential supplies from England were also being offloaded.

As the ship finally docked, a crowd of Newfoundlanders cheered the arrival of the auspicious company. The passengers were out on the deck of the steamer, beaming with pride at the reception. Field, Cooper, Morse and the other passengers waved.

Many of the welcoming party were focused on the appearance of one man in particular: Morse, the man they admired for engineering the telegraph technology. His second wife Sarah and young son accompanied him.

The landing was filled with citizens and politicians, including Governor Charles Henry Darling and the newly elected Prime Minister Phillip Francis Little. Horse-driven carriages were on hand, awaiting the passengers' arrival.

Field had informed them that the island had just conducted its first democratic elections, the start of responsible government in Newfoundland—a step toward independence. That was something the Americans held in common with Newfoundlanders. The influence of the United Kingdom was still visible right there at the King's Wharf: The Union Jack flag—unmistakable emblem of England's sovereignty—flapped in the wind and rain.

Field pointed to it and commented to the others, "It seems so strange, that it, instead of the Stars and Stripes, should be there; for in the forgetfulness of the moment, we supposed we were still under the broad pinion of the American eagle and that Newfoundland was only a distant part of our own republic."

Some of the passengers decided to go touring right away and were impressed with the scenery. Mullaly would later write:

*The roads which branch out in every direction from the
city are without the least exaggeration among the finest
in the world.*

*Beautiful little cottages dot the banks of a river, and
here there may be seen, through the jealous foliage that
cling around them, the more imposing mansions of the
wealthier inhabitants of St. John's. Topsail Road, which
runs along the side of one of the hills that form the
boundary of this valley, affords one of the most delightful
drives in this part of the country.*

That night, festivities began as they were all transported by carriage to the island's legislature, Colonial Building on Military Road. The grand banquet included speeches by colonial governors and elected politicians. Toasts were made about the great adventure ahead of them.

Field was on his feet, raising a glass. "We may be mistaken but we think there was something more than a mere compliment in the hearty response to a toast to the President of the United States. The day may not be far distant that will see Newfoundland bound in closer connection with our republic than can be accomplished by the electric telegraph."

The party continued through the weekend.

The Yankees wanted to return the favour, so they invited 200 locals aboard the *James Adger* for a tour outside the harbour along the rocky coastline. Anyone who was anyone in Newfoundland was on board that spectacular evening.

Who among them there that night could ever have predicted they would be in the presence of such an important man as Morse, on a boat in St. John's harbour no less? The father of the telegraph had been toasted and celebrated in Paris, London, Rome, and New York City. Now they could raise a glass to him in person.

It was a thrill for them to be just a few feet away from the man, listening to him explain how the telegraph instruments worked and translate a message of dots and dashes, using Morse code.

At the time, there was no shortage of skeptics who were unimpressed with the idea of a submarine telegraph project. According to Mullaly, *The Times* in London declared it utterly impractical and that ninety-nine men out of every hundred viewed it as,

the wild project of a Yankee lunatic.

However, on this island, isolated by geography but also strategically located between London and New York City, there was only belief in the transatlantic cable and respect for Field's boldness.

As president, Cooper was impressed by the steadfast support the company had encountered, and commented to the other directors, "They regard the present telegraph enterprise with great confidence, and it will doubtless if successful be attended with the most beneficial effects to them."

Field was grateful the meetings had gone so well and said so during conversations with the company directors, even though he was stating the obvious: "We were most hospitably received by the authorities and citizens of St. John's, who are very anxious to extend their present limited commercial intercourse with us and regard the transatlantic telegraphic enterprise as a powerful means of bringing about such a result."

Newfoundland's politicians, elected and appointed, foresaw that by investing in Field's project, the island would be outfitted with a telegraph network linking it to the mainland of the North American continent and the European continent—including London, where the island's masters still controlled so much of the colony's fate.

The submarine telegraph also had the support of another powerful force in the city: Roman Catholic bishop John

Thomas Mullock. Five years earlier, he had shared his thoughts on the feasibility of an underwater electric cable from Ireland to Newfoundland in a letter to the editor in *The Courier* published on November 8th, 1850.

Mullock had written:

I hope the day is not far distant when St. John's will be the first link in the electric chain which will unite the Old World and the New.

In every plan for the Transatlantic Communication, Halifax is always mentioned, and the natural capabilities of Newfoundland entirely overlooked. Now, would it not be well to call the attention of England and America to the extraordinary capabilities of St. John's, as the nearest telegraphic point?

It is an Atlantic port, lying, I may say, in the track of the ocean steamers, and by establishing it as the American telegraphic station, news could be communicated to the whole American continent forty-eight hours, at least, sooner than by any other route.

Before writing down his thoughts, Mullock had done his research, consulting geographic journals and more, but some facts were not known at the time he wrote that letter. For instance, no one had yet surveyed the ocean floor to find out if it would support a long cable stretching 1,600 nautical miles. That knowledge, which had been discovered in 1853, had propelled them forward, and now here they were on the precipice of a significant change in human communications.

But change was painful and slow—as the New York, Newfoundland and London Telegraph Company directors would learn when they returned to Port aux Basques. The *Sarah L. Bryant* had arrived, and crews had begun the work of laying the cable at the bottom of the ocean between Newfoundland and Cape Breton.

The *James Adger* observed from the water alongside the *Sarah L. Bryant* as the crew laid cable. Almost in slow motion, those aboard the *James Adger* watched in horror as their ship struck the barque. Apparently, Captain Turner was angry with Field about a perceived insult during dinner one evening. He ignored any direction from Field or Cooper.

Then the weather turned foul with gale force winds and heavy seas.

It was impossible to continue work or salvage the situation.

Humiliated, Field and his investors had no choice but to cut the cable and abandon their lofty plans.

The return trip home to New York was a quiet one as the group of businessmen reviewed the failed project. If they were not capable of laying the cable in a body of water the size of a strait, how would they do so in the vast ocean? Their confidence plummeted.

A few months later, Daniel and Helena Craig were enjoying a light lunch at their home in New Jersey when she mentioned *Harper's*, which had just published a report on the excursion to Newfoundland.

"You probably already know most of this, but there's a funny story you may not know about." She offered the magazine to her husband.

Craig took the publication from her hand with raised brows.

"Did you know that there was a veritable dog mania that broke out while they were there?" Helena chuckled.

A puzzled looking Craig opened Harper's, leafed through it, and began reading:

> *A regular dog market was established beside the vessel ...*
> *from morn 'til night with boys and men, each of whom*
> *had from one to five or six pups and dogs. Nearly every*
> *one of our party seemed seized with an uncontrollable*
> *disposition to possess at least one of these dogs while others*
> *still more covetous of canine property purchased whole*
> *families, including large litters of pups.*

The Newfoundland dog normally weighs as much as 170 pounds and stands as high as 30 inches at the shoulder. The massive animal is built for swimming in the icy Atlantic. It has a second layer of fur and webbed feet, making it useful as a working dog and rescuer in the fishing industry.

Most often black in colour, the breed is, as Mullaly described it,

> *majestic, the expression soft and soulful.*

The *James Adger* had left St. John's with forty of the animals on board. Two of the finest were named Telegraph and Cable.

Craig barked a laugh and continued reading aloud:

> *There were dogs on the quarter-deck and dogs forward*
> *and dogs aft. Dogs in every coil of rope and dogs basking*

in the heat of the smokestacks. Pups in boxes and baskets,
pups in berths, puppies in ladies' arms and on ladies' laps.
Go where you want on the steamer, dogs meet you at every
turn. They yelped and they howled, they whined and
barked and through every note of the gamut.

Helena found the whole thing quite hilarious, and they both laughed. "So that is why I've been seeing all these ads this month selling Newfoundland dogs. Ah, the novelty must have worn off. Imagine, a water dog weighing a hundred or more pounds with that thick fur in the city."

"Indeed. The poor things," Daniel agreed. "But you know the dogs may have served a purpose on that return voyage after the devastating failure at Port aux Basques."

Helena stirred her tea. "They certainly were an entertaining distraction by the sounds of it from the article."

In January of 1856, the company tried again to lay the Cabot Strait cable, and this time it achieved what it had set out to do six months earlier. This time, there was no one watching as history was made.

Quietly, the hardworking and diligent staff of the New York, Newfoundland and London Telegraph Company, including Brigus native Thomas D. Scanlan, succeeded in laying the first submarine telegraphic link between the island of Newfoundland and the mainland of North America.

Chapter 11
The Race to the Cape

Craig examined a map of Newfoundland, both hands planted on a large oak table in the NYAP office, blocking out the sounds of the telegraph buzzing with messages. He imagined the telegraph network as it wound its way over hills and through forests of the remote island. He took note of the fact that on the eastern edge of the island, on the Avalon peninsula, Cape Race lay almost due south from St. John's. The distance between the two was about 95 miles, the land curving in and out of a series of bays and coves along the way. Most of the steamships heading to the United States and Lower and Upper Canada from Liverpool charted their course for Cape Race because it was farther south than the capital.

The headland with its dramatically high dark cliffs was the first sighting of land for those ships, making it the obvious location for Craig to station a boat. He had not made it across Cabot Strait to Cape Race himself, so he could only envision the place from the descriptions Gisborne and Field had shared with him after their trip to Newfoundland: the fierce Atlantic Ocean constantly battering the foreboding cliffs, their sharp edges plunging into waves. The ragged ridges of rocks presented great danger to all vulnerable seagoing vessels, from fishing dories to small sailboats to massive longliners. The fog was dense, and crews needed nerves of steel to navigate the area.

Craig had secured exclusive access to the New York, Newfoundland and London Telegraph Company's line to Cape Race as soon as it was operational. It excited him to know he was on the verge of realizing his vision of an NYAP operation at the edge of the North American continent, the first to get its hands on the latest valuable information from abroad.

Craig needed a capable man he could trust to oversee Newfoundland's operation. Initially he had hired a man based in New York. But he quickly realized he needed someone on the ground at Cape Race. He fired his man in New York and sought someone local. Alexander McLellan Mackay was the obvious choice. At the age of twenty-two, the young man from Pictou County had already proven he was capable of running the new Nova Scotia Telegraph Company.

Craig had originally recommended Mackay to Field when he was searching for someone to oversee the laying of the telegraph network across the island of Newfoundland. Field had told him, "We need a man of great strength and capacity to build the telegraph line across the island, more than 600 miles from coast to coast." The first man Field had hired quit in despair after attempting the back-breaking work of clearing the untamed and heavily forested wilderness and turning the felled trees into telegraph poles.

Craig wondered to himself why he hadn't considered Mackay for the NYAP bureau chief in Newfoundland from the start. He met with Field to discuss the idea.

"I would like to appoint Mackay as my top man in Newfoundland. I know he's busy with the telegraph. What are your thoughts?"

Field replied in the affirmative. "I am eternally grateful to you, Daniel, for sending Mackay my way. He's tremendously committed to the telegraph and works as hard as you or me in making progress."

"He's a good man, especially for one so young," Craig replied.

"I imagine Alex can handle both roles without breaking a sweat."

1856 would be a pivotal year for the advance of the telegraph, the NYAP, and Cape Race. Soon after the new year, Mackay travelled by boat from Halifax to Port Aux Basques to begin his new post as superintendent of the New York, Newfoundland and London Telegraph Company..

Despite it being quite possibly the worst time of year on the island, he insisted on travelling from Cape Ray on the west coast through to the capital of St. John's on the east coast, to become acquainted with the geography of the island's interior, as well as with his subordinates and the environment they operated in.

The land was natural, wild, and undeveloped. Travel from St. John's to the outports was done by water, in small vessels and steamers along the coastline around the island. But Mackay was determined as he pushed for progress in an inhospitable landscape. A telegraph operator named A. McQ. Blackadar would write about the difficult task:

> *A line was built through this colony, from Cape Ray on the west coast to St. John's—380 miles; and to build a line through a hilly, watery, and unexplored country like Newfoundland was no small task, but an army of men and mules completed the work in two-and-a-half years.*

Mackay had relied on two men to lead the work and ensure it was done right: John Murphy and Thomas D. Scanlan. The former was believed to be from Cape Breton, the latter was a Newfoundlander from Brigus, where a few years earlier, the very first telegraph line had been laid from St. John's by Gisborne.

A true pioneer, Murphy had worked on clearing the land and the building of the telegraph stations across southern Newfoundland. He, Scanlan, and Mackay were all involved in training the first telegraph operators on the island in Morse code.

Blackadar reflected that on one occasion when Mackay was in the room listening to him and another operator, John Waddell, as they strived to improve their telegraphing skills, he admonished them, "Blackadar, that is an S you make instead of R; increase the space," and "Dwell on them Ls, Waddell, there's no violent hurry. You make Ts of them."

For four months, Murphy trained Blackadar, who worked at the keys every moment he could spare until he was skilled enough to be left on his own.

With Field's approval in hand, Craig sent a telegraph to Mackay in St. John's with a formal offer to take on the role of bureau chief for the NYAP. He was pleased when the offer was accepted.

Now the NYAP truly was set up in Newfoundland and could work on the Cape Race operation. Mackay's first action was to appoint a man he already relied on greatly, John Murphy, to the job of captain and correspondent at Cape Race.

Through the late spring and early summer months, Murphy kept Craig informed of Mackay's progress on the telegraph construction as crews cleared the land from an outport named Cappahayden south to Cape Race through a forested area of balsam fir and black spruce. The tree line then ended abruptly, revealing miles and miles of flat barrens and thick, spongy, marshy land stretching out to the horizon. As they pushed farther south, the telegraph company men carved out a narrow bridle path for the horse and cart to carry the long wooden poles, the cables, and the insulators, which together created the telegraph network.

At the cape itself, twenty men worked tirelessly erecting the first lighthouse to exist at the important headland. It and the incoming telegraph lines generated great excitement among locals who lived along the coast from Cape Race to Portugal Cove South, the nearest outport.

While Mackay was overseeing the telegraph line construction across the island, Field was working from New York and London on the engineering of the lengthy oceanic telegraph cable destined for the bottom of the Atlantic. He was also searching for two ships capable of laying down the heavy cable.

Meanwhile, Murphy and his crew were at the cape figuring out how to make the NYAP operation workable and efficient. As they stood on the headland looking east, Cape Race reached out toward the European continent in welcome, but its shores were treacherous. The ocean currents and wave action were unpredictable. They knew that finding a safe landing site was key if this venture was to be successful. The news boat had to be able to make it to and from the ragged shore on rough seas. It took some time to make it work.

Mackay had hired a team of four strong men to work with Murphy to row for the NYAP news: John Henderson, George Larner, Richard White, and Alfred Gosney. Their only source of power was the will and strength of the four oarsmen to slice through the deep swells, up to sixty feet on stormy days. Often they were on the water for hours, rowing back and forth for the many miles between them and the open ocean.

Upon their return to shore, they had to be clever in navigating a safe landing at one of the two launch pads on either side of the headland. At the east landing, there was a small opening on the beach between two terrifyingly high cliffs, where the men pushed the boat out of the water with brute force. On the west landing, there was no intimidating bluff, but the shoreline consisted of jagged rocks.

Once the boat landed safely, Murphy or one of his crew took off with speed to the telegraph station with the news canisters they had fished out of the heaving seas.

By November, the race to the cape's kinks had been worked out, and Craig was impressed and felt confident in officially launching the Cape Race post. It was not an ideal time of year to do anything on the ocean because it was most often stormy and dangerous for nautical traffic. By necessity, voyages across the ocean slowed down through the dark winter months when weather or icebergs destroyed iron ships. Regardless, Craig was ready to launch the NYAP's news-gathering service on the edge of the continent, after years of imagining it. He felt confident that steamships heading across the violent ocean would soon be stopping at Cape Race to drop off news.

Most steamers already paused at Cape Race for weather information. Those heading for Quebec City and Montreal needed to confirm whether ice was blocking the St. Lawrence River. If that was the case, the liners would steam to Portland, Maine, to drop off passengers and cargo.

On the 5th of November, Craig proudly wrote an announcement that the Cape Race office was open for business and published it in all the newspapers, including the *New York Herald* and *The New York Times*:

*It has been found impossible to get the news yacht of the
New York Associated Press fully equipped until the present
time, but for future she will be found constantly at her
post about eight to ten miles due south of Cape Race light,
and fully equipped for the duty assigned to her.*

*Commanders of steamers and sailing vessels are thus
provided with ready means of communication with the New
York, Newfoundland and London Telegraph offices ...*

Craig predicted a reliable service would lead to a busy period:

Nearly all the European News will be landed at Cape Race.

A month later, in the blackness of December, the Cape
Race Lighthouse shone her light for the first time, providing
safe guidance to ships of all types. William Hally, a retired sea
captain, was appointed the first lighthouse keeper at Cape Race.
He arrived at the southeastern tip of the Avalon peninsula with
his wife, Ellen, and a brood of children. He had an assistant,
George Hewitt. Every evening before dusk, the keeper lit each of
the dozen Argand lamps. During the long dark nights of winter,
Hally and Hewitt took turns visiting the lantern room to ensure
the lamps were still shining. The wind outside could easily send
a draft through the tower, extinguishing the flames. The smoke
was unbearable and, depending on changes in weather, the walls
and tower were either steaming with damp or coated with ice.

Then on Christmas Day, disaster struck at 6:00 p.m., not long
after the family had finished their meal. Hally kept a constant
eye out the window to ensure the light was operating. There

had been a heavy fog all day. He noticed sparks of light cutting through the grey sky.

Grabbing his winter overcoat and a kerosene lamp, he darted outdoors, followed by Hewitt and Michael, Hally's eldest. Distress signals, shooting from just below the headland, where the reefs could be fatal. The men exchanged worried looks.

Returning to the lighthouse, they grabbed ropes and axes and raced back to the edge of the cliff. They looked down to the water's edge, searching for signs of a ship or survivors.

"Hello! Is there anyone down there?" Hally shouted.

Hearing a faint response, they continued to yell encouraging words as they cast a rope down the steep vertical wall of black shale.

"Grab hold of the rope. We'll haul you up."

Three men were rescued on that cold winter night. Despite the trauma of the wreck, they were strong enough to pull themselves up to the top of the cliff. No one said a word as they escorted the men back to the lighthouse. After all the noisy anxiety of the rescue, the silence engrossed them all in their own thoughts.

Ellen had prepared a table of tea with a shot of rum and lassy bread—molasses spread thickly on homemade white bread. Bolstered by the warmth of the fire, the beverages and food, the grateful men recounted the terrible tale of what had occurred.

Their ship, the *Welsford*, had left Saint John, New Brunswick, ten days earlier, loaded with timber and heading for Liverpool. It had lost its bearings and, in the darkness, had rammed into the reefs just beneath the lighthouse on the south side. Twenty-three people were unaccounted for.

The draining energy of grief descended on the group, and the room fell quiet as harsh reality set in.

Hally left to inform the telegraph office. Murphy sent out telegrams to the owners of the steamship, the governor, and the government in St. John's, along with the NYAP.

At headquarters on Broadway, Craig listened to the incoming messages from Cape Race. He noticed immediately the information had been transmitted a mere three hours earlier from Murphy. That gave him a momentary thrill, knowing how quickly he could access information from the northeast corner of the continent.

But as he absorbed the information coming in over the wires, his mood changed quickly. He was saddened to learn of the violent death of the passengers on board the *Welsford*. Craig had been among those who had argued in favour of a lighthouse, believing, as most people did, that it would save lives. But just ten days into its life, it had failed. He was sure everyone involved felt as he did in that moment: frustrated at humans' inability to conquer the power of the fierce North Atlantic Ocean.

Despite the tragic loss, as he ended his day and walked down the stairs, out into the cold winter air, he felt a sense of self-satisfaction and pride as he thought to himself, *The NYAP's arrangement at Cape Race is already proving its value.*

Chapter 12
The First Transatlantic Telegraph

In the summer of 1858, John Murphy, or Captain Jack, was called away from his NYAP duties at Cape Race for a special assignment in Trinity Bay on the northeast coast of the island. Craig had been informed by Field that both of his companies, the New York, Newfoundland and London Telegraph Company. and the Atlantic Telegraph Company, were ready to attempt the monumental task of laying the lengthy wire from Newfoundland to the middle of the ocean and then connecting it with another long cable originating on Valentia Island, Ireland.

Mackay advised Field to use Murphy, his trusted telegraph operator in Newfoundland, to send and receive the first messages coursing along the transatlantic cable between two of the most powerful people in the world: the Queen of England and the President of the United States of America.

Craig had happily agreed to temporarily relieve Murphy of his duties at Cape Race, given the significance of the event taking place. From New York he waited patiently for information from Newfoundland.

Field tasked Mackay with sending out entries from his daily journal to the NYAP offices on Broadway, ensuring that the public would be informed of every stage of the engineering challenge.

The telegraph station was alive with the energy of the era: men engaged in industrious activities working toward progress in a world modernizing, taming the wilderness. It was in a remote part of the globe; no one lived there except for the telegraph operators and engineers and labourers who had constructed the spacious, two-story building with wooden clapboard and more than a dozen windows. On the main floor, the work they were there to focus on took place in the engineer's room and the telegraph room. Both were sparsely furnished with long rectangular wood tables, electric-telegraph instruments, and wires and batteries.

The telegraph house was nicknamed the Cyrus House and had a kitchen with a cook, and eight bedrooms on the second floor for crews to sleep. Often, work conversations continued when they gathered in a sitting room, close to the hearth where a steady fire burned, using the bountiful pine forests surrounding them. Field had plans to install a library and better furnishings so the telegraph operators working there would be more comfortable.

In late July, Murphy was the centre of attention as he sat at a long rectangular wooden table, his hands suspended over the telegraph key, waiting for the leader of the project to tell him which words to create using Morse code, a language he knew well.

Cyrus W. Field stood beside him with a serious expression and began to dictate, "Dear sir, the Atlantic cable, on board the United States frigate *Niagara* and H.B.M. steamer *Agamemnon*, was joined in mid-ocean, July 29th, and has been successfully laid, and as soon as the two ends are connected with the land lines, Queen Victoria will send a message to you, and the cable will be kept free until after your reply has been transmitted."

As Murphy touched the key with finality, cheers erupted among the men standing closely around the telegraph table.

"It is done!" Mackay exclaimed as he slapped Murphy on the back and turned to shake Field's hand.

"Yes!" yelled some of the men witnessing history, while a few stood back in stunned silence. The continents were connected. The transatlantic conversations could begin, ending the isolation everyone had endured.

But it was not yet official. The room went silent as Murphy and the entire crew waited for a message from the Queen, christening the newborn transatlantic telegraph. It would travel from London to Ireland, then across the Atlantic Ocean to Newfoundland and then on to Washington, D.C.

It would be a frustrating two weeks before it arrived on August 16. Always calm under pressure, Murphy received the message. This time he did not pause to partake in the revelry among his bosses, Mackay and Field, and the others in the room.

Murphy was not just a telegraph man; he was an NYAP news agent and his training and instincts prompted him to immediately key the breaking news to Craig, who was waiting anxiously for it to be delivered.

The staff at the offices on Broadway were on standby for this significant dispatch from Newfoundland, and as Craig stood back and listened to it coming in, he did not interrupt them as they moved the information along the telegraph line to their office in Washington, D.C.

It was a lovely summer evening in the American political capital, one so sultry it was sapping everyone of energy, including President Buchanan and some of his cabinet members. The heat was making the sixty-seven-year-old man feel his age as he wiped his brow and rolled up his sleeves. Secretary of the

Treasury Howell Cobb relaxed on the sofa in the White House study along with his colleagues: Secretary of the Interior Jacob Thompson, Secretary of State Lewis Cass, Secretary of War John B. Floyd, Attorney General Jeremiah S. Black, Secretary of the Navy Isaac Toucey, Postmaster General Aaron V. Brown, and Vice President John C. Breckinridge.

Normally after dinner they liked to stand as they smoked cigars and sipped drinks, engaging in spirited discussion about important issues. But tonight, they were all unusually quiet. One by one they removed their formal black vests and jackets and opened the top buttons of their shirts.

The windows were open but the air was as stagnant as the conversation until a welcome interruption occurred. A messenger boy stood at the doorway. Saying nothing, he kept his head down out of respect and walked to the president, a slim slip of paper in his hand. "It's from the New York Associated Press, Mr. President."

Buchanan leaned forward in his chair, eyebrows raised, and took the message into his own hands, scanning it before reading the extraordinary news aloud. In a whisper, he announced that it was from the Queen, about the Atlantic telegraph. Then, louder: "The Queen desires to congratulate the President upon the successful completion of this great international work, in which the Queen has taken the deepest interest."

Cobb shook his head. "It's a hoax."

Thompson agreed. "It must be."

Buchanan wasn't sure what to think. "Well, I recall now, it was just a fortnight ago that Cyrus Field messaged that the two cables had been connected in the middle of the Atlantic."

The others in the room listened and chimed in to a brief debate.

The young boy who had delivered the message stood awkwardly, unsure where to look or what to do.

Then Cobb said, "I don't believe it. We need more confirmation than this short message."

Thompson, the most energetic of the indolent group, stood up and volunteered to get to the bottom of the mystery.

"I will go find Mr. Gobright. It won't be long. The NYAP office isn't far, is it, lad?"

Within an hour, Thompson reappeared, holding the arm of the Washington correspondent as he ushered him into the room toward the president's desk.

Gobright looked around the office where so many important decisions were made every day, and scanned the faces of Buchanan's cabinet. They all looked a little tired and withered from the humidity.

Before he could speak, Buchanan held up the paper with the Queen's message and challenged him, "Is this a hoax?"

Gobright shook his head and smiled in amusement. "No, Mr. President. I received that message myself from my boss Daniel Craig at the headquarters of the New York Associated Press, and he received it from Cyrus Field in Newfoundland, so you can trust its veracity."

Cobbs interrupted, "So it's real. Field and his investors have done it?"

Gobright responded, this time unable to contain his excitement, "Yes, sir. They've connected the continents!"

At that, the seven men got to their feet and gathered closer to Gobright.

Buchanan lowered his eyes, picked up his quill pen, and began writing a reply to be telegraphed across the Atlantic to the Queen of England. It was an historic moment.

*The President cordially reciprocates the congratulations
of her Majesty the Queen, on the success of the great
international enterprise accomplished by the science, skill
and indomitable energy of the two countries.*

*It is a triumph more glorious, because far more useful to
mankind, than was ever won by a conqueror on the field
of battle.*

*May the Atlantic telegraph, under the blessing of Heaven,
prove to be a bond of perpetual peace and friendship
between the kindred nations, and an instrument destined
by Divine Providence to diffuse religion, civilization,
liberty and law throughout the world.*

*In this view, will not all nations of Christendom
spontaneously unite in the declaration that it shall be
forever neutral, and that its communications shall be held
sacred in passing to their places of destination, even in the
midst of hostilities?*

Buchanan finished writing, lifted the paper closer to his eyes, and read what he had written aloud to the cabinet. When he had finished, Cobb looked the president in the eye and said, "Job well done, James! Your words record history."

Gobright reached out his hand to collect the paper. "Thank you, Mr. President. I will make a copy and keep the original."

Buchanan seemed reluctant to let go of the message. Gobright was anxious, thinking of Craig and the Queen waiting for him to get a reply.

Cobb interjected, "It should be placed in the public archives."

Buchanan thought for a moment and then said, "I think the NYAP will keep a good record of it."

"Thank you, Mr. President. I will telegraph this off to Queen Victoria immediately."

Buchanan and his cabinet may have been a little hesitant to believe the breaking news, but when the Queen's message and his own message were printed in all the newspapers served by the NYAP, observers called the transatlantic telegraph the Eighth Wonder of the World.

The extraordinary engineering achievement had proved that communication was possible across thousands of miles of water.

Two weeks later, on the first day of September, a parade moved along Broadway. The city had declared a two-day holiday. New Yorkers, rich and poor, crowded into Lower Manhattan to celebrate. Fifteen thousand spectators packed the sidewalks. Cannons boomed, church bells pealed, and fireworks lit up the sky that night.

The fine autumn day had begun at the Battery at the tip of Manhattan, where medals were awarded to the telegraphic heroes who had backed the transatlantic project. Then it was on to Trinity Church for blessings.

As the parade moved forward slowly, in the next block it passed the NYAP office. Craig stood at the window overlooking Broadway. Seated in the parade's lead carriage were New York City Mayor Daniel F. Tiemann and Cyrus W. Field. A giant coil of the transatlantic cable perched atop a horse-driven flatbed, shaped in a pyramid, a nod to ancient and modern human achievements in engineering. The parade float following the coil of cable was a replica of the USS *Niagara*, the frigate that had laid the cable on the North American side of the project. Six of the actual crew carried the miniature ship, proudly displaying it to the throngs of people on both sides of the street, paying homage to the men of progress behind this remarkable advance in human communication.

The spectators jamming the street cheered. Along the city route, stores and hotels were decorated with banners, placards, and flags. The procession included Highlanders in kilts, pioneers in shakos made of bearskin, butchers in pristine white aprons, veterans of the War of 1812, and even a grand piano—being played. Vessels in port flew the Stars and Stripes and the Union Jack.

The procession travelled northeast on Broadway until Madison Square where the procession swung onto Fifth Ave, following Fifth toward Reservoir Square, the site of the Crystal Palace Exhibition and the ultimate symbol of New York's explosive success. There were speeches, one after another: officials lauding the brilliance of those involved in the Atlantic telegraph project. After the many toasts and cheers, the parade reassembled, and firemen carried 6,000 torches to light the way as it travelled back down Broadway to City Hall Park, where more speeches were made.

Ironically, Morse, the man who invented telegraph technology and brought it to fruition fourteen years earlier, in 1844, was not in the parade. Nor was he in the city for the celebration. He and Field had had a falling out. The same thing had happened to Gisborne, who had brought the project to Field. On the other side of the Atlantic, in Paris, Morse and his wife were feted as that city celebrated the communications breakthrough.

From London to St. John's to New York City, towns and cities held official celebrations with parades and fireworks. Street parties broke out as people on both continents united in their joy. *The New York Times* called it the

most wondrous event of a wondrous age

and declared it had

*solidified New York's position as principal link between
New World and Old.*

Craig wondered to himself what this meant for the NYAP at Cape Race. Would it still be worthwhile having an operation there? If news could be sent quickly under the ocean, was there still an advantage to a news boat at Cape Race? It was something he had to consider.

Within days, he had an answer.

After transmitting 129 messages from Valentia Island to Newfoundland and 271 in the opposite direction, the hopeful cable stopped functioning. It had operated for just twenty-three days. The saltwater had eroded the insulation, short-circuiting the wires and killing the connection.

The Race to the Cape would continue because the transatlantic telegraph had failed.

Chapter 13
The Cape Race Advantage

Craig left the acrid smell of smoke outside as he closed the window in the NYAP office. The clicking sounds of telegraph keys by his staff was familiar—comforting somehow—although the news moving along the telegraph line to the large dingy office was not always positive. In fact, often the paramount stories arriving at the newswire service were distressing. Today's headlines would no doubt be about the source of that burned scent. The blaze was too far north for Craig to determine what was burning.

He called out to no one in particular, "What's on fire?"

A few staff called out over the sound of the telegraph's incoming and outgoing messages, "Crystal Palace. It's destroyed."

That was a surprise to Craig. He had admired the remarkable building with its iron and glass structure. It was only five years ago it had been constructed and everyone, including Craig, had viewed it as a symbol of America's progress. Like most New Yorkers, he had never entertained the possibility it could be destroyed by fire.

Just one month before, it had been the site of the grand party commemorating another great step forward: the transatlantic telegraph. Craig thought to himself it was extraordinary that both achievements had ended in failure. Progress was slower than most men, like himself and Field and his investors, would like.

On the positive side, he was pleased he could continue developing the Cape Race news operation. It had become clear that it might take years to resolve issues preventing the functioning of the Atlantic cable, the key challenge being finding a material that would protect the wires from the salty ocean water.

Craig sent a note to Field, delicately asking him for more news on the project. Would he continue? And how long would it take?

Communication between the continents would remain painfully slow. They had taken a giant leap forward, only to be pushed back to the start. Fast continental conversations across the ocean were again not possible. Men on both sides of the ocean were feverishly working to engineer a new transatlantic telegraph cable system.

As Field and his investors worked on solving problems with the telegraph cable itself, Craig worked on his news post at Cape Race. Geography dictated that European ships heading to Upper and Lower Canada, the colonies, and the eastern seaboard of the United States pass by the treacherous shores on the southeast tip of Newfoundland.

People on both sides of the Atlantic felt a sense of desperation in the search for a solution to their communication challenges; they had glimpsed the potential of the submarine telegraph to connect people, but only for a few weeks. The thought of returning to the old, slow way provoked despondency among many.

The time was ripe for Craig's idea to manifest into a vital service, and a lucrative one. The steamship companies supported it. Canadian shipping magnate Hugh Allan called it a sound idea from the headquarters of the Allan Shipping Line in Montreal. Craig's initial proposal to the NYAP's executive committee had projected an income of $25,000 per year, based on gathering news from twenty-five steamers.

The *New York Herald* would explain that facilities for intercepting steamers off Cape Race had been greatly improved, and steamers bound for Halifax and New York were game for the NYAP's Newfoundland news yachts.

The NYAP advertised with the headline:

Advantage of the Cape Race News Enterprise of the Press.

Craig wrote:

> *By the agency of our news yacht, Cape Race has become*
> *a kind of halfway lookout between this port and Europe*
> *from which persons can receive intelligence from*
> *in-coming and out-going steamers while their voyages are*
> *still uncompleted.*

Craig must have felt satisfied as a growing number of steamers stopped at the NYAP's new post at the end of that long voyage. His life had been tied up with those steamships and the telegraph for more than a decade, from when he and Helena beat everyone else to the news during their time in Boston. He never forgot that his wife's support in the early days of the rowboat news enabled him to build his reputation as an unbeatable newsman.

Craig was known as a calm man amid the highly pressurised era of 1850s New York. He managed to stay composed even under deadline pressure, an essential quality for a reporter. Beneath a balding head were piercing eyes, a passion still driving his ambition, his square jaw set with determination.

His success in transforming the NYAP from a loose coalition of newspapers looking to save money on telegraph fees into an international news agency had given him access to New York's men of progress. He found it entertaining to read about America's status in the world as presented by Abraham Lincoln in a lecture to an audience at the Springfield Library in Amherst, Massachusetts:

> *Young America has ... a great passion—a perfect rage—*
> *for the "new."*

He certainly captured the mindset of the times in New York City and the United States: cocky and confident in the ability of American men to create more and more new inventions, faster, compared with those in England and Europe. Lincoln pointed out a symbol of young America's success: the way men in New York City and Washington were dressed in

> *cotton fabrics from Manchester and Lowell; flax-linen*
> *from Ireland; wool-cloth from [Spain;] silk from France;*
> *furs from the Arctic regions, with a buffalo-robe from the*
> *Rocky Mountains.*

The lecture went on to conjure the image of a bountiful world in the United States.

> *At his table, besides plain bread and meat made at home,*
> *are sugar from Louisiana, coffee and fruits from the*
> *tropics, salt from Turk's Island, fish from Newfoundland,*
> *tea from China, and spices from the Indies.*

Then there were the Cuban cigars from Havana to finish fine meals illuminated by Pacific whale oil, the Brazilian diamond rings, and the gold watches from California where the Gold Rush was well underway.

From the beginning, North Americans compared themselves and their new lives to family and community in England, Ireland, Scotland, Wales, France, and the rest of Europe. The new developments were judged against what had been accomplished back home in the old world—what they had left behind. The drive to be better than the past was a constant. Competition between new and old was part of the struggle to survive.

We have all heard of young America. He is the most current youth of the age. Some think him conceited, and arrogant; but has he not reason to entertain a rather extensive opinion of himself? Is he not the inventor and owner of the present, and sole hope of the future?

Lincoln ended with an acknowledgement of the invention of the telegraph and how it had made young America more powerful than old fogy England.

The lightning stands ready, harnessed to take and bring his tidings in a trifle less than no time. He owns a large part of the world, by right of possessing it; and all the rest by right of wanting it, and intending to have it.

There was no mention of the recent failures by American visionaries. Beneath Lincoln's clever words lay the fact that continental conversations across the Atlantic were not possible, although it had been proven they could occur.

America had not yet conquered the seas.

As the difficult work of engineering the transatlantic telegraph cable proceeded over the next decade, the NYAP news boat at Cape Race helped keep the continents connected.

Chapter 14
The Tin-Can News

One night at Cape Race, around 11:00 p.m., John Henderson stood outside in his Russian overcoat, next to the lighthouse, surveying the ocean for any marine activity. A rower for the NYAP news boat, he was at the ready.

It was eerily quiet—even the birds were sleeping. There was no wind. The sea was dead calm. It was so still he could hear his own heartbeat. The air at the cape felt soft to the skin. A local woman had once told him that the always present fog was good for the complexion. He took a deep breath and exhaled.

Lost in his thoughts about nothing at this late hour, he heard a sound behind him.

As he turned to see who had come out to join him, he was stunned to observe the figure of a man, ghostly and headless.

He watched the man walk off the cliff.

Stories of ghostly apparitions were not uncommon on foggy nights at the cape. Shipwrecks had left many souls exiled far from home, perhaps stuck in a kind of limbo because they died so violently and lay at rest in a watery grave.

The next day, his boss John Murphy—Captain Jack—asked him about what had happened, and after hearing the details of the headless man, Murphy commented, "Be cripes, they are as thick around here as sands in the cove."

On the frontier of the new world, Cape Race could not escape its destiny as a welcome refuge for weary seafaring men and women at the end of a long, often difficult voyage across the Atlantic. The flat, barren headland jutting out into the deep blue ocean was known to shipmasters and sailors around the world. Portuguese fishermen are credited with naming the place in the 1500s after a river mouth in Portugal. Now the Yankees were there, chasing the news—as valuable a commodity as cod had been for centuries.

There was nowhere around the iron-bound coast of sheer cliffs to drop anchor, so the steamships' mail officers filled canisters with important messages and threw them overboard while passing Cape Race. If the water was calm enough during the day, and they had leeway in their schedule, the steamers would stop long enough for Murphy to climb aboard and speak with the captains.

On those rare, fine days when Murphy could climb aboard, the shipmasters greeted him with open arms. Because of the cable across the Gulf of St. Lawrence and the land line to Port aux Basques, he could bring them the latest news—and fresh fish.

Ships passing at night would throw the canisters blindly in the ocean, hoping the NYAP crew would find them. When morning light broke, Murphy and the boys would go fishing for news canisters.

The green, slender cans had small ropes attached to the side and tiny flags, which were meant to assist in finding them as they were tossed around by the waves.

Once the crew spotted a canister in the ocean and rowed close to it, Henderson leaned over the side of the boat and used his rough hands to haul in the fishing line and then he unhooked the jig from the rope on the can with its red flag flapping madly in the wind. The traditional cod-fishing hook used by fishermen was as effective at jigging for news.

"Got ya, ya bloody sleeveen," he yelled as he hauled the ice-cold canister out of the salt water. The catch of the day slipped through his fingers, landing with a bang on the flat bottom of the whaling boat. The five men were not hunting whales today, though. Nor were they fishing for cod, the slippery prey so abundant along the coast of charcoal cliffs of Cape Race.

Just as the mail canister bounced, a huge swell rose and crashed against the side of the boat. Murphy lurched forward, managing to grab hold of the metal missive with both hands. The four other crewmen hung on to the sides, waiting for the swell to subside. The Atlantic seemed more tormented than usual, heaving, sighing, and heaving again: enough to make any man sick to his stomach. But that was nothing new for this crew with well-seasoned sea legs, known from Newfoundland to New York City for their commitment and daring in gathering news.

Within seconds, the five were sitting upright again, not troubled at all by the foggy, windy, rainy weather: just a typical April day in the late 1850s along the southern shore of the Avalon peninsula. Their traditional yellow sou'westers dripped salt water onto their tongues, their oilskin jackets looked as weathered as any fisherman's. From a distance, few would have guessed they were not fishing for cod.

That day there would be no going on board the steamship from Liverpool to chat with the captain and catch up on important news. After throwing the mail overboard, the vessel had continued on its way south to Montreal or Halifax or Boston or New York.

Murphy gave the signal to his crew to turn around and row back to shore where, high above them, the tiny telegraph hut sat beside the towering Cape Race Lighthouse. They grabbed hold of the oars and put their backs into generating enough power to move toward shore, despite the unrelenting waves.

According to Henderson, throughout the day and night, they were on call. "Five men continually on the watch for foreign mail steamers," he would recall. "When any such steamer would heave in sight, we should launch the boat, which when the weather would be rough, was attended with great danger. Some of those steamers would never stop. When near us we would hear someone shout, 'Look out!' and over would go a canister—sealed and containing our mail bag or can on board."

Local fishermen like Patrick Leary, the Molloys, and the Harterys were sometimes called upon to help. If during their day's fishing run they found one of the green canisters, they returned it to the telegraph station and received ten pound sterling—a grand bonus for families in a cashless economy.

Some canisters most certainly got lost, as the process depended on so many elements working together. But the mail itself was well protected. Torches were used to weld the lids watertight.

By hunting canisters among the waves at Cape Race, the NYAP could have the news in New York City in a matter of hours, whereas it could be as many as five days before the ships landed at their destinations on the mainland of North America to deliver the latest in person.

Thomas D. Scanlan was on standby at the hut, anxiously waiting for the crew to return with the mail. He was ready to transmit dozens of messages, if not more. He had his own work orders from the telegraph company to follow: sending private and public messages to clients like the shipmasters in Montreal or the colonial office and government in St. John's.

Murphy focused on telegraphing to Craig and the staff at the NYAP news headquarters. Saving time in disseminating information was the goal of the general manager and the young news service, only a decade old itself. So, shaving off days in the process of gathering news was a huge motivator for shipping companies to plan a stop at Cape Race. Mail delivery was big business. By 1860, steamship companies carrying mail were paid a million pounds a year by the British government.

The telegraph lines were always open, and messages were sent whenever anyone wanted. Operators were on call, especially in distant locations, most of the day. Heavy wave action was a common occurrence and generally was not enough to keep the news boat or the fishermen on shore.

Finding quality men to staff the NYAP's operations at Cape Race had been as important to Craig as hiring his staff in all locations. They had to have marine navigation skills along with telegraphic skills. Murphy was already a legend in the place he had adopted as home because of his strength and skill in the construction and creation of the telegraph network. The work at Cape Race was daring and wild and required men who, like Craig, pushed against obstacles and succeeded in progressing. They played an important role.

Alongside other men of progress engaged in what some would call a demonic chase for speed, some inventors' ambitions drove them to create new life-altering technologies such as the telegraph and the steamship. Both inventions had laid the foundation for the Race to the Cape era. Although lesser known, the men on the frontlines of the telegraphic revolution, such as Scanlan and Murphy, were as eager to be involved and to contribute.

Henderson and the oarsmen were of the same type of character: genuine Newfoundlanders who were proud to be a part of this transformative time in human communications. Hungry to discover more, riding the wave of technological change and making a name for themselves.

Chapter 15
Success at the Cape

In 1861, outside forces once again intervened and delayed the plans and dreams of Daniel Craig, the telegraph visionaries and pioneers, and indeed of all Americans. The Civil War overtook the United States. North against South, the Unionists versus the Confederates. It would split the country, and war news dominated the telegraph lines. The freedom to communicate offered by the telegraph technology since its launch seventeen years earlier was now limited by the demands of military commanders, who had priority on the wires. The conflict slowed down focus on the plans to lay the transatlantic telegraph cable, as the war changed the normal order of things in American society and indeed the world.

In June, a few months after the outbreak of the war, the Galway liner *Prince Albert* glided through the Narrows into the sheltered St. John's Harbour, carrying an urgent message for President Lincoln from Queen Victoria.

Going against the urging of businessmen in England who had an interest in the war, the country had decided not to declare war on the North. Instead, it would remain strictly neutral. This was the kind of news that could change the world, and Lincoln would be grateful to receive it.

The stakes could not have been higher for the small group of telegraph operators in Newfoundland's capital city. They felt that they were responsible for a chance of peace in a significant part of the world.

Unfortunately, technical difficulties meant the news could not be sent: The telegraph lines were down, although no one knew exactly why.

In despair, that Saturday night the operators met at the New York, Newfoundland and London Telegraph Company.'s offices on Water Street to discuss the challenge that lay before them.

"What in God's name are we to do?" said one telegraph man.

Another replied, "I don't see that there's anything we can do. The lines are down."

Another chimed in, "It will take days to get the line from St. John's to La Manche operating again."

Thomas D. Scanlan observed the anxious conversation and said nothing. He was in St. John's to do some relief work at the company headquarters. After much consternation and frustration had been expressed by the group of telegraph pioneers, the authoritative voice of Alexander Mackay, the man running the telegraph in Newfoundland, cut through the din of worried voices. "Don't fall into negative thinking, gentlemen. We have faced greater challenges than this. There's got to be a way."

Then a quiet voice volunteered the crucial message. In an earnest tone, Scanlan convinced them he could get the news through to New York and Washington, D.C. by the end of the next day, regardless of weather or difficulty. The young man from Brigus spoke in a matter-of-fact way, proposing that in order to salvage the situation, they had to get the message to the next working telegraph station, La Manche. As they all knew, it was located more than 80 miles west on the slender isthmus connecting the Avalon to the rest of the island.

Scanlan assured the roomful of nervous men that he could do it. Mackay and the other men listened to the proposal, dubious at first. But Mackay trusted Scanlan implicitly. He had proven his dedication since the beginning of the telegraph construction on the island. If anyone could do this, it was Scanlan.

Mackay looked around the room and then said directly to Scanlan, "Godspeed on this very important journey, Thomas. Britain's neutrality could impact the Civil War. The American people need to hear this news."

Scanlan left St. John's at midnight, with the vital news secured on the inside of a knapsack strapped to his back. At around 2:15 a.m., he arrived at Kelligrews, where he intended to hire a sailboat to cross Conception Bay to Brigus. But the bay was like glass. With no wind, he was forced to walk farther south. He needed a ferry to take him across the bay. But the ferryman was on the other side. Despite yelling until hoarse, he could not get the man's attention. So Scanlan strode onwards until he found a house where he roused a fisherman from sleep, borrowed his rifle, aimed the gun into the sky, and fired a few shots. This worked to alert the ferryman, who then came across to bring him to the other side.

There, the young Scanlan hoped to find a horse and wagon, but had no luck. He walked for a while and eventually found a horse for hire, but after just a few miles, the animal became lame.

"Jesus, Mary, and Joseph in the garden of Eden," Scanlan cursed a blue streak as he encountered one challenge after another. But he did not give up. After a boat ride and then a final three-mile walk to La Manche, the loyal telegraph operator arrived at his destination.

Starving and exhausted from desperately racing against time, but motivated by the knowledge that the fates of nations rested in his hands, Scanlan finally stumbled into the telegraph office at La Manche.

But once again he faced a serious challenge. He discovered the telegraph system itself was not working. Disappointed, he took a few deep breaths and set to work immediately to repair it. As he did so, he was swarmed by voracious mosquitos. Two boys from the settlement stood beside him, waving branches and boughs to keep the insects at bay and provide some relief.

"Thank you, boys. That is a grand help." Scanlan felt grateful for their presence as he fought against time to complete the job.

He sent the fateful words over the line and rested only after he had received confirmation from the NYAP staff in New York that the message had been translated from Morse code and sent on to Washington, D.C.

On Monday morning, the American papers were abuzz with the heartening news from England. Scanlan was declared a hero by his telegraph brethren. His exploits became the stuff of legend as an example of devotion to duty unlike any witnessed before in Newfoundland.

Despite the accolades, the extremes to which telegraph men like Scanlan were willing to go to disseminate news highlighted the fact that the continents of Europe and North America were still profoundly isolated from one another. With an ocean between the two power centres of the world, the war continued for four years, during which human communication was more difficult than ever, despite the remarkable technology now available to people on land.

But the NYAP news boat at Cape Race continued providing a communication hub between London and New York. Craig felt proud as he observed the Cape Race operation flourish. In the 1862 NYAP annual report, Craig detailed the value of the Cape Race news operation, referencing the original proposal he had made four years earlier.

> *Our success at the Cape has been much better the past year than ever before. Indeed, we have doubled the number of steamers boarded at the Cape and have nearly doubled the number of westward bound news steamers. In 1861, we obtained 34 reports. In 1862, about 60.*

> *When the proposition was first made to intercept the steamers at the Cape, you will recollect that twenty-five reports per annum was the height of even Mr. Field's hopes, and for this number, if I recollect right, the Association signified informally its willingness to pay $25,000. During the past year, we have obtained sixty reports for $18,000.*

Craig highlighted that he was able to stick with his initial budget and business plan, keeping staff salaries and costs within the original projections.

> *The salaries of the boatmen and incidentals at the Cape have not exceeded the estimate I gave you in 1859, to wit: $60 American dollars per week. Indeed, the expenses the past year so far as vouchers have been presented do not much exceed $2,000.*

Craig paid senior staff well, as he had promised in his original proposal, suggesting that liberal salaries were required to ensure quality work. He had always asserted that without good quality writers and correspondents, news was just unreliable telegraph information. At the same time, each of the seven newspapers making up the NYAP's board of directors—now including *The New York Times*, formed in 1851—was paying between $60,000 and $100,000 for war correspondents. Clearly the frugal-minded editors were still trying to spend as little as possible on the news service.

However, a weekly pay of sixty American dollars, in cash, was a huge advantage in Cape Race and Portugal Cove South during those years. The income offered Murphy and Scanlan and the other telegraph operators the chance to earn and save money—a freedom not available to the families working in the fisheries.

The colony of Newfoundland was still ruled by England and its merchants controlled the fisheries. Fishermen were compensated by accruing credit at the merchant's store, based on the value of their catch of cod. They were not paid in cash.

By 1863, Cape Race had become a regular stop on the transatlantic crossing routes. The NYAP's operation was doing well. But it was also the focus of some criticism. Concerns were expressed about the risks of the ships slowing down at such a dangerous location. Some argued safety was sacrificed in the obsessive drive to be informed about the latest news as fast as humanly possible.

The Times in London wrote that at Cape Race,

> *In the early summer, when the ice is breaking up and drifting southward, fogs the eye can hardly pierce are almost permanent on the northern coast, and clear days are the exception.*

Scanlan's rush across the Avalon Peninsula, despite every obstacle, had proven the need for reliable communication.

Without it, the war could have taken a drastic turn. The information was worthy of taking the risk, but Newfoundland was just about to find out the true cost.

Chapter 16
Dreadful Marine Disaster

The S.S. *Anglo Saxon* ought to have arrived. It was near noon on Monday April 27, 1863. The fog was so thick, Thomas D. Scanlan was barely able to see a foot in front of him. Even the top of the red-and-white lighthouse towering above him was scarcely visible. He would not likely be able to see the huge steamer offshore. But the eerie silence that accompanied the grey veil meant he should be able to hear the ship's steam whistle. So Scanlan stood still atop the Cape Race cliff at the edge of the North American continent and listened.

And he waited, and he listened. And he waited, and he listened.

All he could hear was the wind and the familiar roar of the waves crashing against the jagged rocks a hundred feet below. The damp, cold air eventually drove him inside the telegraph hut.

He had been employed by the New York, Newfoundland and London Telegraph Company. for nine years now. When Superintendent Mackay had assigned him to Cape Race, he had been twenty-seven and single and had eagerly accepted the assignment working with the telegraphic language that had captivated him since he was a teenager in Brigus.

Inside the small telegraph station, John Murphy sat, restless, ready to jump into action, but patiently occupying himself until then. On this day, neither Scanlan nor Murphy could do their jobs, because the news had not arrived yet.

One of the top liners in the world, the *Anglo Saxon* was a popular transatlantic passenger ship known for its speedy voyages and was on its way home to its base in Montreal, in the Province of Canada. It had departed Liverpool on April 16 and the following day picked up more passengers in Londonderry, Northern Ireland.

The Civil War continued to dominate life in the USA, and the price of cotton stocks was still one of the most valuable and sought-after pieces of information. The cotton textile business in England had been devastated by the instability of the cotton supply as Americans fought to define their nation. Fine linens that covered tables in every kitchen in the United Kingdom hid the truth of the industry built on slavery in the colonies. Day after day, the British consumed their tea and scones on the backs of Black men and women in America. Many were oblivious to the truth. Many more chose to ignore it.

The afternoon at Cape Race was getting long, time seeming to slow down for Scanlan and Murphy with little to do. It was getting near 5:00 p.m. when there was a knock on the door.

Two men stood outside in the miserable weather, looking exhausted and sombre.

The *Anglo Saxon* had wrecked and sunk near a small cove; the men were among the survivors. They had walked for several hours to get to Cape Race.

On this day, these two traumatized men had literally become the news their ship was delivering. Murphy and Scanlan offered them chairs, inviting them to sit down and relieve their weary bodies by the fire. They were given cups of hot steaming tea, drams of rum, and slices of bread slathered with butter.

The *Anglo Saxon* had been caught between two rocks and pounded on her port and starboard sides. The deck had been packed with passengers and crew desperately waiting their turn on the makeshift rope-and-basket system that had been jerry-rigged to get them off the vessel and onto nearby rocks. As far as the men knew, only about eighty-five of 445 passengers and crew had managed to escape death.

Huge swells washed over the ship from stem to stern, and it broke into splinters, throwing those who were still crowded on deck into the sea.

After the wreck sank beneath the unrelenting waves, and with the captain having drowned, chief engineer William McMaster took charge of the scene on shore. Crew members were ordered to gather wooden debris from the wreck and build a fire to warm the shivering survivors. McMaster had directed four men to search for assistance.

They did not know exactly where they had landed, whether north or south of Cape Race, so two men went north from the tiny cove. The two now warming up in the telegraph hut had gone south.

They were uncertain how long they had been walking, but it had felt like an eternity as they stumbled along in the foggy barrens that stretched to the horizon. Eventually they came upon a rise in the spongy marsh and saw the light shining from the Cape Race Lighthouse, offering refuge.

Scanlan hurried to his desk and picked up his well-used electric-telegraph key. He started intently clicking, forming Morse's strange language of dots and dashes, transmitting his first dispatches about the breaking news to the attention of

Superintendent Mackay in St. John's who would pass it on to those who needed to know immediately: authorities in St. John's and the NYAP newsroom in Manhattan.

"Dreadful Marine Disaster" Via Cape Race, April 27, 1863

Wreck of the Steamship Anglo Saxon *Near Cape Race.*

Three Hundred and Sixty Passengers and a Crew of 84 Men on Board.

Murphy and the crew immediately began gathering what would be needed for the rescue. There was no talk of going by sea to find the survivors at what he suspected was Clam Cove. The rescue team was forced to go on foot to the site of the wreck, where once a small community existed, but now it was a tiny beach where no one had reason to visit. Fortunately, there was a four-mile bridle path they could take to get to it, and Murphy knew it well, having helped clear it for the telegraph lines.

Between the fog and the late hour, it was dark enough that they needed kerosene lanterns. The rescuers were strong men. They walked with a determined sense of urgency, and within an hour and a half, they arrived at the headland above Clam Cove, protected on both sides by tall, sheer cliffs, perhaps even higher than those at Cape Race. Murphy guided the group a little inland until he found a more gradual incline to walk down to the beach at sea level.

The tiny lights appearing in the woods behind the sandy beach were met with cheers from the shivering eighty-five survivors. They had despaired of being rescued as they huddled around the fire. They had a short time to recover their bearings before heading out into the dark night to walk back to the lighthouse.

Once there, lighthouse keeper William Hally's wife took charge of caring for the women, children, and some of the men at their living quarters. The rest of the men crowded into the small telegraph hut, some sleeping on the wooden floor in front of the warm fire, others on wooden benches in the work area.

Officers of the ship were required, by law, to make statements as soon as possible after their rescue. At 9:00 p.m., Scanlan was able to send out a more detailed accounting of the disaster. *The New York Times* would report:

> *Seventy-three persons escaped from the wreck by ropes and spars, and 24 more in No. 2 lifeboat, making a total saved of 97. Numbers 4 and 6 boats have not arrived off Cape Race in consequence of the density of the fog, and seven more persons who embarked on a raft, are also missing. There is still a heavy sea and dense fog.*

> *The Commander is supposed to be among the drowned.*

Throughout the wee hours of the morning, Scanlan was overwhelmed with messages as the search effort got underway.

As soon as the news had reached Mackay at the St. John's telegraph office, he informed Craig and kept him updated. Craig gave approval for Mackay's decision to immediately send the tug, the *Dauntless*, south to the scene of the wreck. The sealing ship, the *Bloodhound*, had also been outfitted with coal and supplies in St. John's. Through the night, both vessels steamed south to Cape Race.

People from nearby Portugal Cove South and Trepassey had come to the headland to help as soon as they heard about the wreck, as they had done so many times before. They fired off guns, valiantly sending hopeful signals to survivors still floating on lifeboats in the rough seas around Cape Race.

By 5:00 a.m. the next morning the *Dauntless* had found ten survivors who had spent the frigid night floating on wood from the wreck. One survivor, a crew member, said he despaired of not being seen by the tug, so he hoisted a woman's dress on a piece of wood and waved it until he and the others were spotted. The boat also picked up several people from lifeboats and in the end rescued a total of 113 survivors.

The *Bloodhound* carried the others who had been found. By noon, with 208 survivors rescued, the ships headed north, returning to St. John's where the city residents were waiting to assist.

Word of the disaster had spread overnight and into the morning, neighbour to neighbour in and around Cape Race, and all able-bodied locals gathered to help, some coming on foot across the spongy barren, some by boat, none of them strangers to the deadly power of the sea. That day they dug graves for more than 100 fellow human beings, victims of the worst shipwreck ever on Newfoundland's shores. The region's nickname *the graveyard of the Atlantic* was well deserved. In the end, the final tally of human loss amounted to 237 dead out of a total of 445 souls.

After an exhausting week at Cape Race and St. John's, some uplifting news arrived with the delivery of a letter from the survivors expressing gratitude for saving their lives. Four staff officers—purser William Jenkins, chief engineer William McMaster, second engineer Alex Mackay, and the ship's surgeon Alfred Patton—had written down their appreciation for the Cape Race rescuers' kind efforts to make the rescued passengers and crew more comfortable.

Murphy sent Craig a telegram outlining the events. It put a smile on Craig's face to know that Captain Jack and the entire NYAP crew had received praise for their unselfish effort to assist. Craig was also gratified to see the *Herald* publishing the card of thanks with the headline,

The Press News Arrangements Off Cape Race.

We the undersigned, on behalf of the passengers and crew of the screw steamer Anglo Saxon, *landed on Cape Race, desire to express our heartfelt gratitude for the kindness and unremitting attention of Captain Murphy, Associated News boat; Mr. Scanlan, telegraph operator; Captain Halley [sic.], in charge of the lighthouse; and the men in their service.*

When informed of our disaster Captain Murphy immediately started for Clam Cove, the scene of the wreck ... Our situation on the summit of the cliffs during a dense fog and heavy rain and night coming on, afforded a very cheerless prospect, especially for the women and children, some of whom were nearly naked. Mr. Murphy's appearance was hailed with cheers, and all were soon on the way for the Cape.

Murphy, Scanlan, and the rest of the crew had been elevated to the status of heroes with a celebration of their efforts. The letter of gratitude ended with the heartfelt hope that these gentlemen would have a long, prosperous life. They proposed building a monument to honour the dead at Clam Cove.

Chapter 17
Collateral Damage

The telegraph lines were buzzing with news about the wreck and soon survivors' stories started appearing in newspapers. Craig was obsessed with the story. He picked up a Montreal newspaper topping the pile on his desk, which had a story with the headline,

Graveyard of the Anglo Saxon

It quoted Reverend J.G.K Houghton, a survivor of the wreck and a witness to all that unfolded during the burial of the dead. He chose the word *grotesque* to describe the scene.

Old men and young men were there, two sometimes in one grave, a woman and a child, a man and a youth. It was a terrible sight to see the boats bringing in, now one, now two or three dead bodies, bodies of those who had died in the prime of life or in the full flush of the confidence and the hope of youth, within a few days sail of the land where their friends waited to greet them, or where their new future was laid.

In fact, most of the terror-stricken passengers had been young men, some with families but most single, in their late teens or early twenties and thirties.

Craig was aware that the *Dauntless* had also exhumed the bodies of several women and children, who had been buried on the beach, with clergy like Reverend C.P. Eaton, one of the survivors, having given hasty burial services.

The afternoon the *Anglo Saxon* met its violent end, fifty-three-year-old shipping magnate Hugh Allan was at his home, Raven-scrag, on the slope of Mount Royal in an area known as the Golden Square Mile of Montreal. From the mansion's seventy-five-foot tower, Allan—holding a brass telescope—was scanning the St. Lawrence River for his ships. As each steamer made its way up the winding river, it would transform from a small dot in his scope into a massive ship as it approached the Allan Line wharf.

Allan was as obsessed with speed as Craig. Reducing the time it took for his ships to cross the ocean was a top priority for the company. He lived by the adage that time was money.

The steamers now came weekly from Liverpool to Montreal, and the crossing time had been shortened, making the trip nine days and five hours compared with the twelve to fourteen days it took previously. And the Allan Line had already lost five ships since 1857, recording more than 200 fatalities as ships rushed back and forth, pushing the limits of humans and marine technology.

The Times in London was quick to comment on the disaster at Cape Race, pointing out that the Newfoundland location was well known for hiding in the fog.

The newspaper said that if an iron-bound coast straight ahead, and a dense fog spreading for an unknown number of miles, were not enough to excite caution, then the passengers may as well have entrusted their lives to a captain who sailed by guess.

With no transatlantic telegraph yet, the arrival of the terrible news of the disaster would require a steamship travelling the long distance across the ocean and docking in Ireland or England. The horrific shipwreck and the urgency for communication reinforced the reality that the continents were still not connected. When a ship finally arrived in Liverpool, painful scenes would unfold at the offices of the agents and underwriters when people learned that they had lost a loved one.

The significance of the disaster prompted the *Liverpool Mercury* to publish the names of the people who died and those who survived. It also highlighted Allan's track record in the previous eight years of operation. The worst wreck, the *Hungarian*, killed 205 people just three years before the *Anglo Saxon*.

As soon as NYAP bureau chief Mackay learned the British government had announced an official inquiry, he telegraphed a message to Craig. A magistrate was appointed to oversee the process, and a naval engineer in St. John's was hired to travel to Clam Cove to investigate and present a report in June.

Meanwhile, everyone on both sides of the Atlantic struggled to understand what had happened to cause such a disaster. The newspapers were filled with letters from the concerned public. The debate was intense and lasted until after the inquiry delivered its final report with its conclusions.

A public debate ensued in *The Montreal Gazette*, between Allan and an anonymous critic named Nauticus. Nauticus argued that accidents such as the *Indian* and the *Hungarian* had experienced, were entirely due to the quest to set speed records.

Four years earlier, the *Indian* had sunk with twenty-seven lives lost. Allan had written that financially, Allan Line had suffered the most by far.

He had blamed the passengers for their own deaths, saying that if the steerage passengers hadn't panicked when the ship broke across, and then disregarded all orders, everyone would have survived.

Now, Allan replied to Nauticus that his ships' captains were issued with written instructions to put safety first at all times. He wrote that Captain Burgess had been prohibited from going to Cape Race at night or in foggy weather. However, he had believed that he was far from Cape Race, and that was why he hadn't sounded.

Across the Atlantic in London, *The Times* wrote that it was aggravating to hear praise being bestowed upon the Allan Line shipping company and the captain of the *Anglo Saxon* as the company sought to defend itself in the public realm.

The Anglo Saxon, *we are told, was more strongly built than the ordinary vessels of her class. Her iron plates were of more than the usual thickness, and she was fitted with four watertight bulkheads. The well-constructed vessel, too, was in the hands of a commander of skill and professional knowledge. Captain Burgess is described as a good, very careful navigator, having besides these valuable qualifications, great experience in this particular passenger trade.*

The newspaper placed the blame for shipping disasters on ambition and the push for progress.

*A "quick run" is the besetting temptation and snare of
the commanders of steam vessels. In sailing ships, power
costs nothing, but in steamers to save time is to save fuel,
and coal is money. We fear the disposition to run economy
against safety is not sufficiently discouraged by owners.*

They called the obsession with speed *a childish desire to shorten
a passage* and argued it guaranteed the loss of life if a ship ran
into trouble.

*The precious freight of human life remains, and to the
passengers it is surely of more importance that they should
arrive at their destination safely than that those in
command should dare all hazards and turn common risk
into fatalities to arrive a few hours sooner.*

Carrying on, as the Anglo Saxon *did, in a dense
fog, within a few miles of a rocky coast, ought to be
discouraged by every possible means. It is not skilful, it is
not real seamanship, and it is wilfully defying all lessons
of experience.*

But there were those pointing the finger at the NYAP and
Craig. Critics blamed the practice of dropping off news canisters for many of the wrecks off the Cape Race coast, claiming
that the ships would try to get too near shore in the process and
would get caught in the strong tides.

John Young—then a former cabinet minster and chief
commissioner of public works in the Province of Canada, along
with his wife and seven children, all survivors of the wreck
of the *Anglo Saxon*—and others attacked the British Board
of Trade's policy of requiring steamships to provide lifeboats

exclusively for first-class passengers and crew. The *Anglo Saxon* had six lifeboats, and even if all had been deployed, they would have saved only half the passengers on board.

In New York, Craig and the newspapermen behind the NYAP were closely observing the debates and arguments going back and forth in the newspapers. They had their own opinions and put the blame on the imperial government for not installing a foghorn at Cape Race.

By July, the official report of the Board of Trade's Magisterial Enquiry was presented to the Lords of the Privy Council for Trade in London. It concluded the *Anglo Saxon* wrecked due to the captain's decision not to use a lead to confirm his location off the coast of Cape Race by determining the depth of the water he was steaming through. The lead was a long piece of filmy type material with a weight attached to the bottom. It would be sunk to the far reaches of the sea. If, when they brought it up, it had debris clinging to it, then the captain knew he was close to shore. The inquiry was at a loss to explain why he had failed to utilize it. This was deemed reprehensible and imprudent.

However, they were in no hurry to blame Captain Burgess completely, because he had gone down with his ship, paying the ultimate price for his choices on the voyage.

Neither the Allan Line nor its owner were found at fault.

It was a time in history when capitalists driving the expansion of the shipping industry could do no wrong. Those ships racing across the Atlantic with news and important cargo were vital to the ever-expanding new world. Their power was never more evident than at Clam Cove, Newfoundland, the day after the *Anglo Saxon* wreck.

As the sun had risen above the eastern horizon, the silence of the tiny, isolated cove was broken by the sounds of divers and fishermen chasing after the spoils of the wreck. As it was described in correspondence between the governor and the police chief:

100 boats, small and large, are here at Clam Cove.
Average of 7 men to a boat including divers.

They had come from up and down the Eastern seaboard of North America in search of silver, gold, and anything on the ship that could be salvaged.

Salvage and the money it generated was an integral part of the shipping business due to the frequency of ships wrecking. From Montreal, Hugh Allan telegraphed a request for police intervention to Newfoundland's Governor Alexander Bannerman who refused, saying it would take military might to control 700 men.

Allan had sent his own team of divers and boats to the scene for the salvage operation. He had given permission by letter to his competitor Cunard Lines to do the same. But he did not want average fishermen or wreckers who worked in groups getting access to salvaged goods from his ship. There were laws to protect his property.

But scavenging for lost goods from a shipwreck on the beach was a regular part of life for the honest, hardworking people living along the coast from Portugal Cove South to Cape Race. The locals took advantage of gifts from God, which appeared on beaches and shores: large wax-covered bags protecting essentials such as sugar and flour, furniture, silverware, and gold. Their view was that if the sea was going to take it, they were going to take it instead.

By the end of the summer, things changed at Cape Race. Thomas D. Scanlan departed for St. John's. He moved north and got married. Every morning, he left his home at 65 Prescott Street, at the top of a steep hill, and walked the ten minutes it took to arrive at the telegraph offices on Water Street. The office had more staff and was much busier than the tiny hut at Cape Race, but he was happy to keep busy after the dramatic events of that spring.

He had become Mackay's right-hand man, assistant superintendent of the Anglo-American Telegraph Company, formerly the New York, Newfoundland and London Telegraph Company.

The collective craving for connection through a transatlantic telegraph cable surged. As the telegraph pioneers moved on from the tragedy of the *Anglo Saxon*, the conversation shifted to the transatlantic cable project. Field's company was making progress on both sides of the Atlantic in developing engineering solutions to the durability of the cable and the process of laying two wires and connecting them mid-ocean.

At the NYAP, the news agency continued to grow and expand, but it was already well established and a permanent player in the news media in North America. Craig was content. The NYAP was the international wire service he had imagined when he began in 1850. Cape Race was a feather in his cap. Pulling off a daring rowboat news chase that gave him first access to the foreign news was nothing short of genius, according to some observers. Others called it bizarre.

The Civil War finally ended, to the relief of most Americans. They could all return to their lives, although much had changed as a result of the conflict.

The NYAP had newspaper clients in all the major American cities now. The western states had grown and expanded in the previous sixteen years. Craig was hearing from editors that they wanted more than just New York oriented news.

He was trying to determine how to handle that demand in the summer of 1866, when the transatlantic telegraph breakthrough they had all been waiting for occurred in Heart's Content, Newfoundland and Valentia Island, Ireland. The dream of a cable uniting the old and new worlds had come true, after twelve long, frustrating years. Its completion would change everything.

Chapter 18
End of an Era

The exuberant parade moved slowly up Broadway, winding its way north, an expression of victory over the enemy known as distance. New York City was celebrating the second success of the transatlantic cable, eight years after the initial success and failure of the mammoth project. New Yorkers crowded the sidewalks, cheering for this true breakthrough in long-distance communication across the ocean. The insulation on the cables had been fortified and the issues with too high voltage, which degraded the insulation further, remedied.

The noise distracted Daniel Craig from his work at the NYAP headquarters and he stood at the fourth-floor window overlooking Broadway, observing the throng of people and their enthusiasm. The continents of North America and Europe were now connected, and Americans were proud of their involvement in this great stride toward a modern world where communications would be easy and fast. They were cheering the end of isolation.

Reflecting on earlier times and struggles, when fighting waves and wind in a rowboat, pigeons in baskets at his feet, chasing the impossible, the fifty-four-year-old NYAP boss felt pride for what he had accomplished since he had taken over sixteen years earlier. The NYAP now had a monopoly on national news and was firmly centrist in ideology, while Americans started seeing themselves as part of the nation as a whole.

The parade signalled to the world that life was about to change because technology was advancing once again. Attitudes—whether toward diplomacy or the gathering of news—had to be overhauled completely.

A trumpet player hit a high note and jarred Craig back to the present moment. He noted to himself that the festivities were not as loud nor as long as compared with the parade eight years earlier, when New York and the world had gone wild at the first, yet short-lived, success of the transatlantic telegraph project. When it failed after only a couple of weeks, many citizens felt foolish for having believed the continents could be connected by a thin wire. They were embarrassed by their jubilant expressions of pride.

This time, Craig sensed New Yorkers were tempering their excitement somewhat, in the event the cable failed again. But he trusted that this time the cable across the Atlantic would hold.

From that very first night at Cyrus Field's house when the project was launched, Craig had confidence that Field would succeed. He felt certain that in 1866, the triumph of man over nature would be permanent, considering the extraordinary effort and intelligence that had been applied to this challenge by engineers, innovators, and telecommunications companies on both sides of the ocean.

The monstrous steamship, the *Great Eastern*, had laid a submarine telegraph wire covered in a new material—gutta-percha—to protect the electrical signals from water as they moved along the line. The cable had reunited the British and American people. As *The Times* in London put it:

*The Atlantic is dried up and we become, in reality as well
as in wish, "one country."*

Now, messages were flying through the cable connecting
North America to Valentia Island, Ireland. The green isle was
already technologically connected by cable to England.

The London newspaper compared the laying of the submarine
cable to the discovery of the new world:

> *Since the discovery of Columbus, nothing has been done in
> any degree comparable to the vast enlargement which has
> thus been given to the sphere of human activity.*

Telegraph pioneers in New York City, Newfoundland, and
London were all impressed at this expansion in human communication. As Charles Frederick Briggs and Augustus Maverick
wrote in their 1858 book *The Story Of The Telegraph: And A
History Of The Great Atlantic Cable*:

> *The laying of the telegraph cable is regarded, and most
> justly, as the greatest event in the present century: Now the
> great work is complete, the whole earth will be belted with
> electric current, palpitating with human thoughts and
> emotions. It shows nothing is impossible to man.*

Most observers believed the technology would naturally lead
to harmony on earth. Briggs and Maverick added:

> *It is impossible that old prejudices and hostilities should
> longer exist, while such an instrument has been created for
> the exchange of thought between all nations on earth.*

A sense of national pride was in the air that day as surely as electrical energy is always there in the atmosphere waiting to be harnessed. The world of human communication had evolved further, and now the language of business, government, and personal relationships could flit across the bottom of the ocean, a concept that so many had been unable to conceive. A permanent change in all spheres of life.

But as with the land telegraph, the news media was most affected by this technological advance. News editors like Craig and Bennett were delighted to be able to rely on the news arriving from England and Europe in a timely manner.

They no longer had to endure long wait times to receive vital information about life and business on the European continent. It inevitably sped up the pace of communications just as the land telegraph had sparked speedy messages back and forth across the telegraph lines.

New York City was an industrious expanding metropolis in 1866. Craig reflected on how much the city had changed. The bustle was more intense, the crowds thicker. The wires strung between telegraph poles were now interlaced through the branches of shade trees along Broadway. They carried an onslaught of messages, translated in and transmitted from the telegraph office by workers labouring ten hours a day, six days a week. Women were employed alongside men because they had proved quick learners on the telegraph and companies could legally pay them a lower wage.

Things had also changed at the NYAP—for the better, Craig believed. His original plan, mapped out in 1850 to demonstrate to the board what exactly the newswire could look like, had come to fruition.

Correspondents for the service were collecting and reporting the news in fact-based dispatches fired across the telegraph network to all corners of the United States and British North America. Those working in the news business were always on watch to check that reports were unbiased and did not represent the beliefs, opinions, or wishes of any specific person. This was central to what the NYAP was—and later, what the Associated Press would be.

Craig's instincts about the benefits of expanding the NYAP beyond paying consolidated telegraph fees to include staff reporters across the country and coordinating with newspapers beyond the six founders in New York, proved worthy. The emergence of the Associated Press as a prominent supplier of national news was an indication of the progress the United States was making in nation building.

By 1856, when the telegraph lines reached Cape Race, the merging of many smaller telegraph companies into only a few major conglomerates enabled the NYAP to run a well-oiled system to distribute information to the press all over the nation.

And now, a decade later, the transatlantic telegraph system seemed to signal a brand-new beginning in media, eclipsing the great expansion which occurred after the land telegraph in 1844. News editors were now empowered by easier communication between the old world and the new. Continental conversations constantly coursed along the telegraph line lying at the bottom of the Atlantic. But beginnings infer endings, and this step forward in human communications also meant the end of the Race to the Cape era.

Cape Race's extraordinary role as the news nexus between New York City and London was usurped by the transatlantic cable. There was no need any longer for a dangerous race to the cape to deliver news faster to Daniel Craig and the NYAP.

The rowboat news at Cape Race had had an incredible run. John Murphy had become a legend among telegraph and news people. He would make it into the island's history books, admired for his daring and strength. Murphy just hadn't expected to become a part of the past so soon. Craig regretted having to inform him and his four-man crew that their services were no longer required at the edge of the continent—that their days chasing steamships for news were done. He telegraphed a note of thanks, releasing both Murphy and Mackay from their duties as NYAP's chief correspondent and bureau chief respectively.

In a surprising twist, two months later, things irrevocably changed for Craig too.

The dissatisfaction of the directors of the Western Associated Press with the NYAP service had set events in motion. As telegraph lines and railway tracks had expanded west, western newspaper owners and editors demanded more from the NYAP. They wanted stories about their own experiences, not just what was happening in the east. They wanted telegraph reports to be reliable above else, to be as brief as possible, and for information to be of interest to the subscribing newspapers and not because it was important to New York readers.

Craig was trying to find a way to appease the western editors. But the directors on the board in New York were loath to give up any of the power it had accumulated. They refused to make any changes to keep the complaining editors happy.

The western men stubbornly dug in their heels and refused to give up their quest for better, more relevant news for their newspapers.

Rumours began circulating that Craig was at odds with the men dictating the policies in New York. Tensions were building.

The directors who had believed in him in 1850 had been replaced with a new generation of news editors. The *Herald*'s James Gordon Bennett Sr. was no longer there; his son James Gordon Bennett Jr. had taken over. Joseph P. Beach was manager of *The Sun* now, having replaced his father, Moses Yale Beach.

Sixteen years after joining the NYAP, Craig, with his unbeatable and daring methods, no longer impressed his bosses. On November 5, the shocking news broke for the man who had been called the monarch of news gathering. The board fired off a brief telegraph message to every client of the NYAP.

Daniel Craig is discharged by unanimous vote of the members.

There was no explanation. No praise for the work he had done in creating the newswire. Just a few dots and dashes spelling the end for Craig, sent out two days after his fifty-fifth birthday.

The message also announced that James W. Simonton would replace Craig. If the latter was affected in any way by the sudden turn of events, he certainly hid it well. Instead, it seemed to trigger his competitive energy and, as always, the ambitious newsman did not miss a beat.

He rented an office in the same building and immediately tapped out a telegraph message of his own, claiming the NYAP information was *utterly and infamously false*. He surprised everyone by revealing he had submitted his letter of resignation several weeks before.

Craig also announced he was starting his own news service and encouraged the NYAP clients to switch their business to his operation: the United States and Europe Telegraph News Association.

Initial reports were that he was still as capable as always.

The western editors designated Craig the general agent of the Western Associated Press.

The rift between the NYAP and Craig, who was sympathetic to the desires of the western news editors, presented an opening for Murat Halstead of *The Commercial* in Cincinnati and Horace White from the *Chicago Tribune* to assert their demands in person. They travelled to New York to meet with the directors and protested the limited approach to news gathering. They threatened to move all their business to Craig's service.

A period of cutthroat competition ensued in which Craig and his replacement at the NYAP transmitted complete reports, day and night. The NYAP's agents in other cities were bombarded by both sides, and for a month, they barely knew who they served.

Observers criticized the Western Associated Press's decision to part ways with the NYAP, accusing the western editors of courting destruction, but they soon had a change of heart. Craig was as skillful as ever, and his reports were superior.

Then the first real break in solidarity with the NYAP occurred when one of its clients took the side of the the western editors. The *New York World* was the first publication to withdraw its membership from the NYAP news service. This was when the shaken New York majority ordered all its own news reports withheld from papers using Craig's service.

Craig fired back, notifying his subscribers that if they took service from the New York Associated Press, they could not continue to receive the western news budget as well.

New York redoubled its attacks, insinuating sabotage by Craig. When Lincoln's successor, President Andrew Johnson, addressed a hostile Congress that December, trees were felled across the wires being used by Craig to transmit the news. Once again there was no actual evidence of Craig doing anything criminal, like chopping down trees or cutting lines.

A heated two weeks in the competition for news finally ended when, behind closed doors, the directors at the NYAP and the editors from the Western Associated Press met secretly. They negotiated a new deal that would give the western papers what they wanted: news about more than the narrow interests of New Yorkers. The New York Associated Press would soon become the Associated Press.

Craig was then let go from the Western Associated Press. He had been sacrificed by both groups in favour of the new agreement they signed on January 11.

Interestingly, the man the NYAP had selected to replace Craig would also be let go. One of the the terms of the treaty was that, for the sake of harmony, Simonton would also retire.

As the middle-aged Craig walked down the long, still dimly lit stairway on the corner of Broadway and Liberty Street for the final time, he felt bitter and disillusioned.

He meandered in the dark along a familiar pathway back to his home in New Jersey. The snow was falling hard enough that it slowed him down, and he breathed in the cold air of winter as he tried to absorb what had just occurred. As he focused on his feet, watching them take one step at a time, he felt the weight of the brutal ending. He was in no hurry to get home on this dark day and deliver the news to Helena, his constant support throughout his pioneering work in journalism.

Craig's career had always travelled in an upwards trajectory. He had built one success on top of another and moved confidently through the world. But in a bizarre twist in his own story, he was now unemployed, rejected by the very organization he had created with the sheer force of his will and imagination.

Losing his title and power at both the NYAP and now the Western Associated Press, Craig was shocked by his downfall. He had not seen it coming—unusual for him, a man who had always been viewed as someone who was on top of what was happening in the new business, a visionary. Yet here he was. The extraordinary, unbeatable news maverick was beaten.

Epilogue

Daniel Craig retired and lived in Asbury Park, New Jersey, for the rest of his life with Helena. His children lived nearby. Neither followed in their father's footsteps into the news business, and there were no descendants to carry forward the story of Craig's contribution to journalism, from carrier pigeons to transforming the NYAP.

The man who was such a driving force in the expansion of journalism was forgotten as time and technology marched on. His role in the creation of the enduring newswire service would fade into history. But his legacy in journalism lives on: those two principles of objectivity and fact-based news.

On January 5, 1895, Craig was at home, sitting upright in a chair, when he experienced a fatal heart attack. He was eighty-one.

In the grief-filled days following Craig's passing, his wife of sixty-one years found solace visiting their daughter Ida. The women were comforted to read the newspaper editorials that praised the *Pioneer News-Gatherer*, as *The Sun* in Baltimore called Craig, for his contribution to journalism in America.

Mr. Craig was the first manager of the original Associated Press, the parent and the pattern of all subsequent news-gathering associations. He was the originator of fast news

service in the United States, a field in which his efforts predate
the introduction of the electric telegraph by a few years.

News editors throughout the country recalled the legendary days when Craig travelled undercover from Halifax to Boston on the *Herald*'s steamer, the *Buena Vista*, and the significance of what he had done.

Helena's eyes welled up as she remembered the fun she and Daniel had on the wharf in Boston.

Captain John Murphy, who was at the centre of the Race to the Cape, married a woman from St. John's, Susan Mills, in November of 1863. Archival records could not confirm what happened to this daring and courageous man.

The four rowers at Cape Race would continue working on the Newfoundland telegraph, repairing the network of lines stretched across the island: Larner in Pushthrough, White in White Bear Bay, Gosney in an unidentified location, and Henderson in Grandy's Brook and then Burgeo. Henderson married my great-grandfather Daniel Leary's first cousin, Susan Curtis.

Thomas D. Scanlan continued to work for the Anglo-American Telegraph Company in downtown St. John's for the rest of his life. One summer day, at age fifty-eight, he lay down on the sofa and passed away peacefully in his sleep at his home on Rennie's Mill Road. He had returned from an excursion with his family, around the bay to his summer home in Brigus, where he had consumed his final Sunday dinner.

Alexander Mackay adopted Newfoundland as his home and spent the rest of his life on the island. After retiring from the telegraph business, he entered provincial politics, winning a seat in the legislature representing the Burgeo region along the south coast.

In 1844, the telegraph represented the greatest revolution in communications since the development of the printing press. One hundred and fifty years later, the internet sparked a wildly expansive time, not dissimilar from the impact of the telegraph.

In April 2013, the co-inventor of the internet, Vinton Cerf, wrote in the foreword to Tom Standage's book *The Victorian Internet: The Remarkable Story of the Telegraph and the Nineteenth Century's Online Pioneers*, that modern internet users inherited the telegraphic tradition. Like the telegraph, modern social media is built around two-way communication of short messages, sent and received instantly. People used the novel telegraph technology as madly as they use the internet today. They visited the telegraph office to send quick messages to loved ones simply because they could. But within a short period, the telegraph messaging system became clogged with unimportant or inaccurate messages, as Craig had detailed in his early campaign to set a higher standard for news reports at the NYAP.

The usefulness of being so connected comes with downsides, and Cerf wrote that we need to remain mindful of these, along with being optimistic and enthusiastic.

Daniel H. Craig might turn over in his grave to learn of the changes that have occurred in the field of journalism in the twenty-first century. He might think the state of news has regressed, to a time when newspapers were owned by wealthy men who used the platform to share their opinionated view of the world, not for the public good, but for profits.

He did not respect such journalism. The news reporter in him always valued objective information, reported in an unbiased manner and not expounded upon to please a specific clientele. From his own experience, he knew what was required. And when the NYAP gave him the chance to hire good men to work for him, he hired employees who wanted to raise the standard of news reporting.

The invention of the telegraph changed the journalism landscape irrevocably and created technology-driven media. Craig and the New York newspapers behind the NYAP were front and centre in that period of development. They were the minds who created something entirely new, unheard of before: a newswire service that distributed its information reports for many newspapers at the same time, based on facts and an objective mindset.

As time marched on, the NYAP continued to grow as an international newswire service, but neither it nor Craig received much attention from historians writing about media in the United States. Most observers focused on newspapers in the early days when journalism was developing as a valued profession, and Associated Press wire reports were seldom included in writings on the journalism, the newspapers, and the editors of the era.

And yet objective news reporting was practised by news reporters throughout North America since the 1850s. It was at the NYAP that the discipline of approaching all news from the curious mindset of someone who knows nothing and has no biases became institutionalized.

It is not 100 percent foolproof, but the practice has worked well for most journalists trying to tell true stories since the heady days when the telegraph news morphed into the NYAP news.

The AP continues to exist, and in 2024 it celebrated its 178th birthday.

Its byline can be seen from capitals around the globe, still providing accurate, objective news for newspapers and broadcast networks.

The O'Learys—or Learys, as they were known—as well as the Molloy, the Hartery, and the Coombs families still live at Portugal Cove South. The community remains tiny, with only 150–200 residents. The fishing community is quieter these days, with the cod fishery moratorium in 1992 ending a way of life for Newfoundland families. Tourism is the new industry bringing people to the cove now.

A UNESCO World Heritage Site is located at Mistaken Point, between the cove and Cape Race. The fossil site consists of a narrow strip, seventeen kilometres in length, of rugged coastal cliffs. These cliffs are of deep marine origin and date to the Ediacaran Period—580–560 million years ago—representing the oldest known large fossils anywhere.

These fossils represent a watershed in the history of life on Earth: the appearance of large, biologically complex organisms, after nearly three billion years of evolution dominated by microbes.

Newfoundland's pioneering telegraph-communications history and its location continued to place the island in the sights of inventors of communications systems. At the turn of the twentieth century, Marconi arrived in Newfoundland, pursuing the next technological advance: wireless telegraph. The Italian inventor wanted to move thought and words along electric lines without cables and wires under the Atlantic Ocean. From Signal Hill, St. John's, Marconi sent out his signal and connected with ships travelling across the ocean. The Marconi wireless station at Cape Race lasted for decades.

Radio was the next focus. During World War II, Cape Race would be used by the United States as a key location. Canadian government radar and weather stations operated at Cape Race for decades.

Cape Race endures as first landfall in North America for ships from Europe, offering assistance to mariners in trouble and signalling the end of the long sea voyage.

The lighthouse, a national historic site, continues as an Atlantic sentinel, dominating the skyline at the southeastern tip of the Avalon Peninsula. No one lives there now. Two lighthouse keepers take turns maintaining the light. It is machine operated, so they only go inside to maintain the machinery that keeps the light going twenty-four hours a day.

A replica of the old telegraph hut is now a museum, capturing the area's telegraph and communications history. The Myrick Wireless Interpretation Centre is named after the Myricks, the courageous family who replaced the Hallys and lived and worked on keeping the light burning at Cape Race for decades.

The telegraph key belonging to Great Aunt Kitty sits proudly in the welcome exhibit at the entrance, a nod to the beginning of technology at Cape Race.

Nothing marks the graves of those buried at Clam Cove except a small cardboard historic storyboard. No memorial was ever constructed, although many of the survivors proposed it in the days after the tragic wreck of the *Anglo Saxon*.

The cliffs are as dark and foreboding as ever.

The fog remains as thick as pea soup on most days of the year.

The sea is as tormented as ever.

Author's Note

My dad had left the cove as an infant, but his visits there as a youngster with his parents were a thrill, and he retained so many stories about the cove and Cape Race. He passed that love onto me, and now here I am, writing this story.

One of my first childhood memories is driving into Portugal Cove South on the dusty, gravel road. It was a beautiful sunny day. We kids wanted out, so Dad stopped the vehicle and out sprang a crowd of youngsters—not sure if all eight of us were there on that trip. The air was so fresh, the sun was shining, the blue ocean was sparkling as the light hit the salt water. This was foreign to me as a girl growing up far from the sea in Labrador. I felt like I was in a special place.

The three youngest, me included, stayed at our great uncle John Molloy's with his wife, Aunt Josephine—who everyone called Phine, so we did too. She was a tall woman to me, and she had such a big heart. I have always cherished that visit. She gave us lots of attention. As kids in a large family, being singled out for special attention was rare. She tucked us into bed that night. She kept piling heavy wool blankets on the bed, to the point we could not move. We giggled. Luckily sleep came quickly, as it does to children after a day outdoors in the warm sunshine and fresh salty air of the ocean.

I do not know the origins of my family in Ireland, except they came from County Cork. What I do know is that records show Patrick Leary on the southern shore of the Avalon Peninsula in Newfoundland in 1787. Patrick, his son or grandson, was born in Trepassey in 1808. Patrick the junior married Catherine Ryan, and they lived in Portugal Cove South. Their son Daniel—my great-grandfather—was born in Portugal Cove South in 1844. He married Mary Corrigan, and they had a crowd of children. Their eldest daughter, Great Aunt Kitty, was born in Portugal Cove South in 1882.

I have always wondered where my great-grandparents Daniel and Mary learned Morse code and the operation of the electric-telegraph keys. My research led me to conclude that Daniel learned the skills first at the telegraph hut at Cape Race during those visits in the months and years following the installation of the telegraph station. By the time Daniel was thirty-four, he and Mary were operating the post office from their home in Portugal Cove South, across from the beach, in the centre of town. Mary trained her eldest daughter, Kit, in the telegraph, and Kit then passed on the knowledge to her youngest sibling, my granddad Jim.

At age thirty, Kit, an energetic, hard-working, devout Roman-Catholic woman who was known as a force, married Frank Lahey and moved north to Cape Broyle, where she continued to work as a telegraph operator for the political Cashin family.

As the telegraph networks expanded, companies came to realize women were as quick to learn Morse code and the operation of the telegraph keys. And they were cheaper to employ due to specific labour laws. Regardless of what opened the door to women in the new field of telegraph communications, it was a starting point for many girls and women to work as telegraph operators, news correspondents, and communications workers.

It seems my great aunt Kitty, who I admired since childhood, was skilled enough and smart enough to find work in the new world the telegraph was creating. Family lore claims that she was at Cape Race the night the *Titanic* went down. Officially there are no records to prove that, so perhaps it is simply one of those boastful family stories. There is a local rumour though that a woman was there that night, and that she ran from the lighthouse to the telegraph hut, where she sent out messages to alert the world. Some have speculated it was one of the Myrick daughters who lived at the lighthouse in 1912. The girls were nicknamed Dot and Dash, and it seems likely they knew how to operate the Cape Race telegraph. But could Kit have been there? Her descendants never heard her talk of the *Titanic*, but telegraph operators were sworn to secrecy by their employers.

Years later, Frank Dalton remembers his grandmother, Kit, sitting at the table in her kitchen with the telegraph set so she could hear the news being transmitted about World War II. Fishing boats heading to the Grand Banks of Newfoundland would stop in at Cape Broyle to get bait and the news from Great Aunt Kitty. She could translate the sound of the dots and dashes from listening to them and would read them out loud as the messages were coming in. A radio broadcaster before radio broadcasting existed.

Grandad Jim married Maggie Molloy in Portugal Cove South. Their third son, Paul Joseph, was born in 1931, and a month later, the O'Learys left their beloved cove with my dad in his mother's arms.

They moved for work, managing Newfoundland Railway stations first in Norris Arm, then in St. George's during World War II, and finally in Grand Falls-Windsor. Jim O'Leary's telegraph skills, learned from his older sister and mother, had opened doors for him just like they did his father.

Growing up in Wabush, Labrador, a land-locked iron-ore mining town far from the Atlantic Ocean, I sensed my father's yearning for his beloved cove. He would often say, "I was born ten feet from the sea," with such pride and love of place and his ancestors.

I find it ironic that my chosen career was a news reporter on the radio, the technology that followed the telegraph in creating technology-driven news media. Perhaps it was fate.

It was not my intention to be a journalist. But by age twenty-one, the first news report I ever wrote went to air on CBC Radio in St. John's, Newfoundland—about the creation of the now infamous cobblestone road George Street. I had an hour's training in radio, and somehow, with the help of a patient co-worker, managed to piece together a story coherent enough to end up on the airwaves.

No one was more shocked than me to hear my voice on the radio in March 1983, but it turned out I had a voice that was meant for that service. My deepest gratitude to my ancestors for that stroke of luck.

A few historical mentions are necessary at this point.

The use of the term *new world* to describe North America is not meant in any way to diminish the reality that Indigenous people inhabited the land for centuries and millennia. For the sake of providing context in this book, the term will be used.

No archeological research has yet uncovered Indigenous visitation or settlements at Cape Race, but farther north along the east coast of Newfoundland at Ferryland, it has been confirmed that Beothuk families spent time there. Small fireplaces made of circular piles of stones, with charcoal, discarded food, and potential stone tools were found there, though no sign of permanent housing was reported.

Fragments of sixteenth century Portuguese-manufactured Merida ware—two handled stone jars—were also discovered in the same layer of the earth as the Beothuk hearths.

From the 1500s, Portuguese fishermen spent their summers in Newfoundland, naming one of their fishing stations, the one on the southern shore of the Avalon peninsula, Portugal Cove South, so as to distinguish it from Portugal Cove, farther north near St. John's.

The White Fleet is credited with naming Cape Race after a cape at the mouth of the Tagus River in Portugal. The Basque, the English, and the French were also sending migratory fishermen to the area during the 1500s, 1600s, and 1700s.

Maury's Plateau was mentioned, having been discovered in 1853 by Matthew Fontaine Maury and his team and deemed an excellent place to lay a cable between Newfoundland and Ireland. There has since been doubt cast on the accuracy of Maury's findings. Nevertheless, at the time, decisions about the transatlantic telegraph cable were based on Maury's work.

For context, it was only in 1867, one year after the Atlantic cable success, that Canada became a country, initially a federation of four provinces: Nova Scotia and New Brunswick, Ontario, and Quebec. Newfoundland did not join Canada until 1949, eighty-two years after the country was formed.

Fifty years after the *Anglo Saxon* wreck, the *Titanic* wrecked about 400 miles off the coast. On April 15, 1912, Cape Race received the first distress call from the worst shipwreck ever, which took the lives of around 1,500 innocent people. There were not enough lifeboats for all passengers. The British govern-ment had still refused to make it mandatory for ships to provide safety vessels for those not in first class.

Acknowledgements

I could not have completed this labour of love without the assistance of librarians and staff archivists at the following institutions and groups: Vancouver Public Library and the Kitsilano branch, The Rooms Archives in St. John's, Memorial University Centre for Newfoundland Studies and Digital Archives, the Nova Scotia Archives, McGill University Archives, Library and Archives Canada, BAnQ–Bibliothèque et Archives nationales du Québec, the Hampshire Genealogical Society, the Rumney Historical Society in New Hampshire, and the New York Public Library, especially the staff in the Rare Book Division.

Thank you also to the AP Corporate Archives staff for providing me with some archival material and for connecting me with the author of *News Over the Wires*, a book about the AP in its early days based on access to the AP's archives. Professor Menahem Blondheim's enthusiastic response to the news I was researching a book that would feature Daniel Craig as the main character inspired me.

A special thanks to Bob Moulton for providing me with the names of three of the four oarsmen: a gift that appeared out of nowhere, answering a question I was desperate to answer. And thank you to Andy Jones for giving me an 1855 copy of *Harper's*, with the story of the trip to Newfoundland.

Thank you to Donald Sedgwick, former executive director, King's College MFA program in Halifax, for giving me the title for this book and affirming it was a story worth uncovering. I am also grateful to colleague and friend Kim Kierans for opening that door and providing housing.

Thank you to historian and one of Canada's best-known nonfiction writers, Charlotte Gray, for being a positive support throughout the lengthy process of writing the book. Her encouragement to keep going helped a great deal—more than she will ever know. Her reminder to not go down too many rabbit holes of research was especially good advice.

It takes a village to raise a new author, so my deep gratitude to all those wonderful souls who believed in me and loved books enough to really care. I won't forget.

Many dear friends, colleagues, and supporters contributed to a GoFundMe campaign to get me from BC to Newfoundland and New York City to do crucial research. Others helped with research or accommodation. Thank you to Mary Frances Keating, Trudie Richards, Tom Flynn, Karen Tankard, Kathy Shaw, Leigh Milroy, Mea (Marie) Hutchison, Mark Forsythe, Chris Throne, Joan Athey, Geoffrey Davies, Marie Normore, Wayne Comeau, Nina Winham and her late mother Linda Winham, Rosemary Alder, Robert Moulton, Michael Davidson, Elinor Benjamin, Toula Hatziioannou, Sheila Moores, Rod and Leanne Dobbin, Sandra Watts, Meranda Squires, Ruth Lawrence, Sylvie Zebroff, Sonya Jampolsky, Jim Knock, Maureen Brosnahan, Angeline Higgins, Steve Athey, Bernard Graham, Susan Elrington, Nancy Roach, Karmela Briggs, Catherine Buckie, Marina Macdonald, Andrea Goldsmith, Yvonne Gall, Vicki Gilbert, Devon Query, Susan McNamee, Karl Wells, Karin Konstantynowicz, Susan Cardinal, Laura Lynch, Tina Pomroy, Lorna Haeber, Michael Bradley and Peter Alteen, Ranza Clark, and David Kyle.

Deep thanks go to my late dear friend Susan Cardinal—a top CBC Radio journalist in Canada, a cherished colleague and mentor who taught me so much about journalism and story-telling—for her editorial input on the book. She even painted a painting for me to honour the project.

I must thank my late father, Paul Joseph O'Leary, for passing on the stories from the cove, which piqued my curiosity and led to the writing of this book. Our love of storytelling was a bond that endured until his death in March 2020.

He was thrilled to know his beloved cove would be remembered through my stories from his stories. Thanks also go to my late mother, Frances Barnes-O'Leary, who was my biggest fan when I stepped into the world of radio news at age 21, and who lived vicariously through me during my adventures on the chase for a news story across Canada and the United States.

I am also deeply grateful to my 90-year-old aunt Theresa McCullough, Dad's sister, for always believing in me, loving me unconditionally, and getting me back to NL at a critical moment.

Thank you to my sister, Helen, for providing family photos and information and my brother, Paul, for photos of Great Aunt Kitty and her telegraph keys, and for creating the family tree.

I would like to acknowledge my ancestors: grandparents James (Jim) and Margaret (Maggie) Molloy; great-grandparents Daniel and Mary (née Corrigan) O'Leary or Leary; beloved great aunt Phine (Josephine) and uncle Tom Molloy; Patrick and Catherine (née Ryan) Leary or O'Leary, first generation born in Newfoundland; and Patrick's father, Patrick O'Leary from Cork, Ireland, who arrived on the southern shore of the Avalon Peninsula of Newfoundland in the late 1700s.

A sincere thank you to all of the residents of Portugal Cove South and Trepassey for allowing me to share this incredible story that took place on their shores. I remain humbled by the fact that I get to tell this story. Through the years, I thought for sure someone might have done so.

I am also so grateful to my cousins and relatives who live in Portugal Cove South and Renews for their open hearts and willingness to share stories of the past with me, especially Brendan and the late Marie O'Leary, who generously invited me to stay with her during my research; Joe O'Leary; Jennifer O'Leary-Ready; June Coombs; Francis Molloy; Kit Ward; Mary-Frances Keating; and Mayor Clarence Molloy, among others. Special thanks to Brandon Ward and his Facebook page. Portugal Cove South Genealogy provided me with invaluable photos and stories and worthwhile information. Clifford Doran, a former Cape Race Lighthouse keeper, was also extremely helpful.

Race to the Cape would not have been possible to complete over the past nine years without the emotional, financial, housing and/or editorial support of these special people: Lisa Cordasco, Darryl Jackson, James Hubbard, Elaine Janes, Karl Wells and Larry Kelly, Elaine Janes, Vickye Herrington, Vic Addison, Susan McNamee, Lorna Haeber, Leigh Milroy, Vicki and Brent Gilbert, Theresa Taaffe, Wendy Cook, Rosemary and Paul Wayvon, Meranda Squires, Lillian Bouzane, Bruce Wark, Patricia Hartery, Beth Ryan, Mark Forsythe, David Plewis, Laura Lynch, and Del and Shirley Phillips.

As a national and international news journalist for more than three decades, I have told thousands of stories, varying in length from a one-minute radio news story to hour-long radio documentaries. I have written for television news, the web, and magazines. I wrote, directed, and produced a comedic stage play and a short tragic film. But this book of creative nonfiction is the most challenging story I have ever told.

I am grateful to author Marie Beswick-Arthur for introducing *Race to the Cape* to Ingenium Books Publisher Boni Wagner-Stafford and editors Amie McCracken and Linell van Hoepen. Thank you for supporting me every step of the way as I transitioned from journalist to historic nonfiction author.

Bibliography

"237 Lives Lost: Total Wreck of the Anglo Saxon 1863." County Londonderry. Accessed June 2025. https://cotyrone.com/colondonderry/ships/AngloSaxonWreck1863.html.

"Advantage of the Cape Race News Enterprise of the Press." *New York Herald.* September 20, 1860.

"Dreadful Marine Disaster." *New York Times.* April 27, 1863.

"The Loss of the Anglo Saxon." *The Day-Book.* June 12, 1863.

"Total Wreck of the Anglo Saxon 1863." *Liverpool Mercury.* May 11, 1863. Old Mersey Times, 2002. https://www.old-merseytimes.co.uk/ANGLOSAXON.html.

Appleton, Thomas E. *Ravenscrag: The Allan Royal Mail Line.* McClellan & Stewart, 1974.

Bannerman, Governor, and Police Chief Mitchell. Correspondence. The Rooms Archives, St. John's, Newfoundland and Labrador.

Blondheim, Menahem. *News over the Wires: The Telegraph and the Flow of Public Information in America, 1844-1897.* Harvard University Press, 1994.

Briggs, Charles F. and Augustus Maverick. *The Story Of The Telegraph: And A History Of The Great Atlantic Cable (1858).* Kessinger Publishing, 2010.

Burrows, Edwin G. *The Finest Building in America: The New York Crystal Palace, 1853-1858.* Oxford University Press, 2018.

Craig, Daniel H. Letter to George R. Young, Member of the Nova Scotia Legislature for Pictou County. May 2, 1851. MG2, vol. 723, F2, no. 971, Nova Scotia Archives.

Daniel Craig's obituary. *The Baltimore Sun.* January 7, 1895.

Darrow, L.R. Letter from the New Brunswick Electric Telegraph Company. December 8, 1849. Nova Scotia History Digital Preservation Initiative.

Gramling, Oliver. *Associated Press: Story of the News.* J.J. Little and Ives Company, 1940.

Johnson, Arthur and Paul Johnson. *The Tragic Wreck of the Anglo Saxon, April 27th, 1863.* Harry Cuff Publications, 1995.

Kinsella, Payson J. "Newfoundlanders—Three." *Newfoundland Quarterly.* December 1901.

Lincoln, Abraham. Abraham Lincoln Online, 2020. https://www.abrahamlincolnonline.org/lincoln/speeches/discoveries.htm.

Meaney, J.T. "Communication in Newfoundland." *The Book of Newfoundland.* Volume 1. Newfoundland Book Publishers, 1937.

Mullaly, John. *A Trip to Newfoundland, Its Scenery And Fisheries; With An Account Of The Laying Of The Submarine Telegraph Cable.* T. W. Strong, 1855.

"News Yacht Off Cape Race—European News." *New York Times.* November 6, 1857.

NYAP Annual Report, 1862. NYAP Archives.

Pitts, Jonathan M. "The rising Sun: How A.S. Abell launched the paper in 1837." *The Baltimore Sun.* Updated March 2, 2025. https://www.baltimoresun.com/2012/05/08/the-rising-sun/.

Prowse, Daniel W. *A History of Newfoundland, from the English, Colonial, and Foreign Records.* Dicks & Company Ltd, 1971.

Rasmussen, Frederick N. "Samuel F.B. Morse gave the first public telegraph demonstration 178 years ago in Baltimore. The federal government was less than impressed." *The Baltimore Sun*. June 2, 2022. https://www.baltimoresun.com/2022/06/02/samuel-fb-morse-gave-the-first-public-telegraph-demonstration-178-years-ago-in-baltimore-the-federal-government-was-less-than-impressed/.

Regan, John W. "Nova Scotia Pony Express 1849: The Beginning of the Associated Press." Library and Archives Canada. Latest revision January 21, 2002. https://epe.lac-bac.gc.ca/100/205/300/nova_scotias_electric_scrapbook/07-04-09/ns1763.ca/ponyexpress/ponyex01.html?nodisclaimer.

Schwarzlose, Richard A. "The Formative Years, From Pretelegraph to 1865." *The Nation's Newsbrokers*. Volume 1. Northwestern University Press, 1989.

Silverman, Kenneth. *Lightning Man: The Accursed Life of Samuel F.B. Morse*. Alfred A. Knopf/Random House, Inc. & Toronto: Random House of Canada Limited, 2003.

Smallwood, Joseph R.. "Thomas D. Scanlan's Great Exploit." *The Book of Newfoundland*. Volume 3. Newfoundland Book Publishers, 1967.

Standage, Tom. *The Victorian Internet: The Remarkable Story of the Telegraph and the Nineteenth Century's On-line Pioneers*. Bloomsbury USA, 1998.

The Barrelman Radio Program Papers. St. John's Scripts, July 1–31, 1949. COLL-028, 1.01.132. Archives and Special Collections, Memorial University of Newfoundland.

The History of the Abell Family. Reynolds Historical Genealogy Collection. Gc 929.2 Ab3406 2042584, 1913.

About the Author

Even though she grew up in Wabush, Labrador, Theresa M. O'Leary knew Cape Race on Newfoundland's Avalon Peninsula well. Her father's Irish ancestors had settled in nearby Portugal Cove South and some, like her great aunt Kitty, worked at the Cape Race telegraph station.

Perhaps it was fate that Theresa would become a journalist on the radio—the technology that followed the telegraph in getting the news to the people. She has won multiple awards for her work with CBC National Radio News for daily reporting and her documentaries. She is also a playwright and filmmaker.

You Might Also Enjoy ...

The 49th Protocol

ingeniumbooks.com/49P

12 Elephants and a Dragon:
A Memoir of Survival
and the Kindness of Strangers

"Honest, heartfelt,
harrowing, and beautiful."
Nguyen Thieu An, writer, Under the Squash Vine

12

A Memoir of
Survival and the
Kindness of Strangers

ELEPHANTS
AND A
DRAGON

Dr. Vi Tu Banh
with Marie Beswick Arthur

ingeniumbooks.com/12ED

Flying
With Dad
Yvonne Caputo

A Daughter. A Father.
And the Hidden Gifts in His
Stories from WWII.

"Captivating!"
— Jane LaTour, *Sisters in the Brotherhoods*

A "...moving story."
— James Bradley, *Flags of Our Fathers*

ingeniumbooks.com/Flying

"UNFORGETTABLE PROSE, MASTERFULLY COMPOSED."
CORA TAYLOR, AWARD-WINNING AUTHOR OF *JULIE* AND *SUMMER OF THE MAD MONK*

LITERARY TITAN
BOOK AWARD

MARIE BESWICK ARTHUR

LISTEN FOR WATER

ingeniumbooks.com/lfwp

Leaving the Safe Harbor:
The Risks and Rewards of Raising a Family on a Boat

ingeniumbooks.com/LTSH

www.ingramcontent.com/pod-product-compliance
Lightning Source LLC
Chambersburg PA
CBHW031506120626
46545CB00005B/1771